The Science of Political Economy

Abridged Edition

Condensed by Lindy Davies

Henry George

Robert Schalkenbach Foundation

Henry George

The Science of Political Economy

Henry George

RSF

ROBERT SCHALKENBACH
FOUNDATION

ROBERT SCHALKENBACH FOUNDATION
New York City
2020

The Science of Political Economy

Abridged Edition

Author: Henry George
Condensed by Lindy Davies
Book ISBN: 978-1-952489-00-6
Robert Schalkenbach Foundation

Official Publishers of the works of Henry George

Cover Image
by Marcus P. on Unsplash

Robert Schalkenbach Foundation
info@schalkenbach.org
www.schalkenbach.org

This book was produced with the support and cooperation of the Henry George School of Social Science and the Henry George Institute.

Special thanks to Harry Pollard for contributing the introduction, to Mike Curtis and Mark A. Sullivan for editorial guidance, and to Chuck Metalitz and his students for proofreading.

The Robert Schalkenbach Foundation (RSF) is a private operating foundation, founded in 1925, to promote public awareness of the social philosophy and economic reforms advocated by famed 19th century thinker and activist, Henry George.

Today, RSF remains true to its founding doctrine, and through efforts focused on education, communities, outreach, and publishing, works to create a world in which all people are afforded the basic necessities of life and the natural world is protected for generations to come.

Contents

Foreword:
The People's Economic Scientist

by Harry Pollard

He was a high school dropout who spurned the Chair of Economics at the University of California. He was a job printer, but handily defeated Teddy Roosevelt in a mayoralty contest for the city of New York.

Leo Tolstoy read him, realized the significance of what he wrote and tried to persuade the Czar of Russia to adopt his ideas before it was too late. The Czar did not warm to Tolstoy's plea — and soon it *was* too late.

He was known around the world. The Irish enthusiastically cheered his speeches. Australia and New Zealand introduced his ideas of taxation to much of their territory, as did Canada's West Coast.

Sun Yat-Sen, called "The Father of Modern China", read him and declared that the path for China would be his "decentralist economic ideas". Sun's thinking influenced the Taiwanese, who introduced widespread land reform based on his economic writings. The theories were confirmed by practice. Farm production increased so much that Taiwan, with a population density of more than 1,300 to the square mile, achieved a net export of food. *The London Economist* said that the "miracle of Taiwan" rested on this successful land reform.

Perhaps his greatest influence was found in Britain at the beginning of the 20th century. Liberal Party policy looked as if it had been copied from his many books. Churchill declared he had made speeches by the yard endorsing and promoting this self-taught economist's policy of taxing land values.

At that time, the greatest obstacle to any meaningful legislation was the House of Lords. The land of Britain was almost entirely held by fewer than 3,000 landholders — who controlled the Lords. That unelected body could nullify any legislation passed by the elected House of Commons.

So, the Liberal Party forced the issue. They put forward the Parliament Bill, a measure that would cut the claws of the Lords. With the aid of the Bishops, who sat in the House of Lords, the Parliament Bill passed by a scant 15 votes. The veto power of the House of Lords was ended. They could no longer prevent the enactment of a general tax on land value. This law was passed in 1913, and the process began.

Unfortunately, "the war to end all wars", WWI, began the following year — and that ended the land value tax legislation. As part of the price for supporting the war, the Tories demanded that all controversial legislation be stopped. The process of assessment and collection of the land value tax was ended and it was never resumed.

The Parliament Bill remains in force until this day, however. For the last century the House of Lords have been unable to interfere with any money bill.

They were tumultuous times — and a brash Philadelphian named Henry George was in the middle of the tumult, because he had the nerve to write clear, comprehensible books on how the economy works.

He entered the scene with *Progress and Poverty*, published in 1879. After a slow start it took hold and millions of copies were sold. It was a book of economics like no other. He questioned everything. His opening shot showed the intention of his thinking: "Why do wages tend to a minimum that will give but a bare living?"

It is striking that more than a century later, the question is no longer asked in modern economics. The modern War on Poverty has already been lost and its soldiers spend their time treating the casualties.

Such failure was not good enough for George. Again and again he hammered home a query. Why, he wanted to know, with the enormous increase in the power to produce, is it so hard to make a living?

He was, perhaps, the first labor economist, but one who did not mince his words as he discussed wages and unemployment. "Why are people looking for jobs," he thundered, "Why are not jobs looking for people?"

His concern for the condition of labor did not blind him to the need for scientific methodology. He began correctly at the beginning, by carefully defining the basic terms of economic science. Not for him the loose meanings that lead to loose thinking. During this process he was properly unkind to icons in the science such as Adam Smith, David Ricardo and John Stuart Mill, demonstrating how their less than accurate use of terms sent them on false journeys.

George did his job properly. He began with a concept and defined it, which meant putting a fence around it. He then placed a label on the things within the fence. When he had finished, he had terms that contained within them everything on earth — indeed, everything in the universe. There was no fence-straddling. There would be no confusion in the language of his new study, which he named *The Science of Political Economy.*

His study did not lean on the use of mathematics. Rather, he relied on everyday language, so that all his theories could be understood by anyone who could read. This meant that his reasoning was clear and could be accepted, or attacked, by any thinking person.

The attacks came from those at whom his finger pointed.

Yet, overwhelmingly, his books achieved acceptance and wielded influence around the world.

Even to the present — for when Russia dispensed with communism, eight Nobel Prize-winning economists wrote a letter to the president suggesting that Russia's basic problems could be dealt with by application of the ideas of Henry George. At the moment in Britain, discussion of George's ideas can be heard from local town councils to Parliament.

The Science of Political Economy draws on his thinking from several books. Within this volume is synthesized the essence of economics as a science. His ability to move from the simple to the complex, connecting every point by a mixture of logic and observation, lays before us a canvas that shows us the whole picture.

Henry George died before the book was completed. The original publication was finished by the author's son from notes. In this new edition, Lindy Davies has carefully edited and tightened the manuscript to provide us with a work of which the author would have approved.

Harry Pollard has been teaching the science of political economy for more than fifty years. He has taught in the classroom, on radio and television, and in public forums. He is the author of the popular Inter-Student *Economic Courses, which have been widely used in California high schools since the 1970s.*

Introduction; Reason of this Work

I shall try in this work to put in clear and systematic form the main principles of political economy.

The place I would take is not that of a teacher, who states what is to be believed, but rather that of a guide, who points out what by looking is to be seen. So far from asking the reader blindly to follow me, I would urge him to accept no statement that he himself can doubt, and to adopt no conclusion untested by his own reason.

This I say, not in unfelt deprecation of myself nor in idle compliment to the reader, but because of the nature and present condition of political economy.

Of all the sciences, political economy is that to which civilized men of today is of the most practical importance. For it is a science which treats of the nature of wealth and the laws of its production and distribution; that is to say, of matters which absorb the larger part of the thought and effort of the vast majority of us — the getting of a living. It includes in its domain the greater part of those vexed questions which lie at the bottom of our politics and legislation, of our social and governmental theories, and even, in larger measure than may at first be supposed, of our philosophies and religions. It is a science to which must belong the solving of problems that are in all civilized countries clouding the horizon of the future — the only science that can enable our civilization to escape already threatening catastrophe.

Yet, surpassing in its practical importance as political economy is, he who today would form clear and sure ideas of what it really teaches must form them for himself. For there is no body of accepted truth, no consensus of recognized authority, that he may without question accept. In all other branches of knowledge properly called science the inquirer may find certain fundamentals recognized by all and disputed by none who profess it, which he may safely take to embody the information and experience of his time. But, despite its long cultivation and the multitude of its professors, he cannot yet find this in political economy. If he accepts the teaching of one writer or one school, it will be to find it denied by other writers and other schools. This is not merely true of the more complex and delicate questions, but the primary questions. Even on matters such as in other sciences have long since been settled, he who today looks for guidance of general acceptance in political economy will find a chaos of discordant opinions. So far indeed are first principles from being agreed on, that it is still a matter of hot dispute whether protection or free trade is most conducive to prosperity — a question that in political economy ought to be capable of as certain an answer as in hydrodynamics the question of whether a ship ought to be broader than she is long, or longer than she is broad.

But while this discordance shows that he who would really acquaint himself with political economy cannot rely upon authority, there is in it nothing to discourage the hope that he who will use his own reason in the honest search for truth may attain firm and clear conclusions.

For in the supreme practical importance of political economy he may see the reason that has kept and still keeps it in dispute. Under existing conditions in the civilized world, the great struggle among men is for the possession of wealth. Would it not then be irrational to expect that the science which treats of the production and distribution of wealth should be exempt from the influence of that struggle? Macaulay has well said that if any large pecuniary interest were concerned in disputing the attraction of gravitation, that most obvious of all facts would not yet be accepted. What, then, can we look for in the teaching of a science which directly concerns the most powerful of "vested rights" — which deals with rent and wages and interest, with taxes and tariffs, with privileges and franchises and subsidies, with currencies and land tenures and public debts, with the ideas on which trade unions are based and the pleas by which combinations of capitalists are defended? Economic truth, under existing conditions, has not merely to overcome the inertia of indolence or habit; it is in its very nature subject to suppressions and distortions from the influence of the most powerful and vigilant interests. It has not merely to make its way; it must constantly stand on guard.

It is especially true today that all large political questions are at bottom economic questions. In the study of theology, the same disturbing element has written in blood a long page in the world's history — and at one time, at least, it so affected even the study of astronomy as to prevent the authoritative recognition of the earth's movement around the sun.

Colleges and universities and similar institutions, though ostensibly organized for careful investigation and the honest promulgation of truth, cannot be exempt from the influences that disturb the study of political economy. For in the present social conditions of the civilized world nothing is clearer than that there is some deep and widespread wrong in the distribution, if not in the production, of wealth. To disclose this is the task of political economy, and a really faithful and honest explication of the science must disclose it.

But no matter what the injustice may be, colleges and universities, as at present constituted, are by the very law of their being precluded from discovering or revealing it. For no matter what the nature of this injustice, the wealthy class must, relatively at least, profit by it, and this is the class whose views and wishes dominate in colleges and universities. As, while slavery was yet strong, we might have looked in vain to the colleges and universities in our Southern states, and indeed for that matter in the North, for any admission of its injustice, so under present conditions we must look in vain to such sources for any faithful treatment of political economy. Whoever accepts from them a chair of political economy must do so under the implied stipulation that he shall not really find what it is his professional business to look for.

In these extraneous difficulties, and not in any difficulty inherent in political economy itself, lies the reason why he who would really know what it teaches can find no body of doctrine that he may safely accept.

Yet if political economy be the one science that cannot safely be left to specialists, the one science of which it is needful for all to know something, it is also the science which the ordinary man may most easily study. It requires no tools, no apparatus, no special learning. The phenomena which it investigates need not be sought for in laboratories or libraries; they lie about us, and are constantly thrust upon us. The principles on which it builds are truths of which we are all conscious, and on which in everyday matters we constantly base our reasoning and our actions. And its processes, which consist mainly in analysis, require only care in distinguishing what is essential from what is merely accidental.

In proposing to my readers to go with me in an attempt to work at the main principles of political economy, I am not asking them to think of matters they have never thought of before, but merely think of them in a careful and systematic way. For we all have some sort of political economy. Men may honestly confess an ignorance of astronomy, of chemistry, of geology, of philology, but few honestly confess an ignorance of political economy. Though they may admit or even proclaim ignorance, they do not really feel it. There are many who say that they know nothing of political economy — many indeed do not know what the term means. Yet these very men hold with the utmost confidence opinions upon matters such as the causes which affect wages and prices and profits, the effects of tariffs, the influence of labor-saving machinery, the function and proper substance of money, the reason of "hard times" or "good times," and so on. For men living in society must have some sort of politico-economic theories — good or bad, right or wrong. The way to make sure that these theories are correct, or if they are not correct, to supplant them by true theories, is by such systematic and careful investigation as in this work I propose.

But to such investigation there is one thing so necessary, one thing of such primary and constant importance, but I cannot too soon and strongly urge it upon the reader. It is, that in attempting the study of political economy we should first of all, and at every step, make sure of the meaning of the words that we use as its terms, so that when we use them they shall always have for us the same meaning.

Words are the signs or tokens by which in speech or writing we communicate our thoughts to one another. To understand one another with precision, it is necessary that each attach precisely the same meaning to the same word. Thus, two men may look on the ocean from the same place, and one honestly insist that there are three ships in sight, while the other as honestly insist that there only two, if the one uses the word "ship" in its general meaning of navigable vessel, and the other uses it in its technical meaning of a vessel carrying three square-rigged masts. Such use of words and somewhat different senses is peculiarly dangerous in philosophic discussion.

But words are more than the means by which we communicate our thoughts. There also signs or tokens in which we ourselves think — the labels of the thought-drawers or pigeonholes in which we stow away the various ideas that we often mentally deal with by label. Thus, we cannot think with precision unless in our own minds we use words with precision. This is especially important in political economy, for in other studies most of the words used as terms are peculiar to that study. The terms used in chemistry, for instance, are used only in chemistry. But the terms used in political economy are not words reserved to it. They are words in everyday use, which the necessities of daily life constantly require us to give to, and accept for, a different than the economic meaning. In studying political economy, in thinking out any of its problems, it is absolutely necessary to give to such terms as wealth, value, capital, land, labor, rent, interest, wages, money, and so on, a precise meaning; and to use them only in this — a meaning which always differs, and in some cases differs widely, from the common meaning. But not only have we all been accustomed in the first place to use these words in their common meanings; but even after we have given them as politico-economic terms a definite meaning, we must, in ordinary talk and reading continue to use and accept them in their ordinary sense.

Hence arises in political economy a liability to confusion in thought from lack of definiteness in the use of terms. The most eminent writers on political economy have given examples of this, confusing themselves as well as their readers. To guard against this danger it is necessary to be careful in beginning, and continuously to be careful. I shall therefore in this work try to define each term as it arises, and thereafter, when using it as an economic term, try to use it in that precise sense, and no other.

To define a word is to mark off what it includes from what it does not include — to make it in our minds, as it were, clear and sharp on its edges — so that it will always stand for the same thing or things, not at one time more and at another time less.

Thus, beginning at the beginnings, let us consider the nature and scope of political economy, that we may see its origin and meaning, what it includes and what it does not include. If in this I ask the reader to go with me deeper than writers on political economy usually do, let him not think me wandering from the subject. He who would build a towering structure of brick and stone, that in stress and strain will stand firm and plumb, digs for its foundation to solid rock.

Part I — The Meaning of Political Economy

Chapter 1 — Man and The World

In the world — I use the term in its philosophic sense of the aggregate or system of things of which we are cognizant and of which we ourselves are part — we are enabled by analysis to distinguish three elements or factors: 1) That which feels, perceives, thinks, wills; which to distinguish, we call mind or soul or spirit. 2) That which has mass or weight, and extension or form; which to distinguish, we call matter. 3) That which acting on matter produces movement; which to distinguish, we call motion or force or energy.

We cannot, in truth, directly recognize energy apart from matter; nor matter without some manifestation of energy; nor mind or spirit unconjoined with matter and motion. For consciousness itself begins with us only after bodily life has already begun, and memory by which alone we can recall past consciousness is later still in appearing. It may be that what we call matter is but a form of energy; and it may perhaps be that what we call energy is but a manifestation of what we call mind or soul or spirit; and some have even held that from matter and its inherent powers all else originates. Yet though it may be that at bottom they are one, we are compelled in thought to distinguish these three as independent, separable elements. Of these from our standpoint, that which feels, perceives, thinks, wills, comes first in order of priority, for it is this which is first in our own consciousness, and it is only through this that we have consciousness of any other existence. In this, as our own consciousness testifies, is the initiative of all our own motions and movements, so far as consciousness and memory shed light.

We awake to consciousness to find ourselves, clothed in flesh, and in company with other like beings, resting on what seems to us a plane surface. Above us, when the clouds do not conceal them, the sun shines by day and the moon and stars by night. Of what this place is, and our relations to it, we could individually know little more than is presented to us in direct consciousness, little more in fact than the animals know. But the observations and reflections of many succeeding men, garnered and systematized, enable us to know things to which the senses untaught by reason are blind.

By the light of this gathered knowledge we behold ourselves on the surface of a globe seemingly fixed, but really in constant motion of many different kinds — a globe large to us, yet only as a grain of sand on the seashore compared with the bodies and spaces of the universe of which it is a part. We find ourselves on the surface of this ceaselessly moving globe, as passengers, brought there in utter insensibility, they do not how or whence, might find themselves on the deck of ship, moving they know not where, and who see in the distance similar ships, whether tenanted or how tenanted they can only guess. The immeasurably great lies beyond us, and about and beneath us the immeasurably small. The microscope reveals infinitudes no less startling to our minds than does the telescope.

Here we are, depth upon depth about us, confined to the bottom of that sea of air which envelops the surface of this moving globe. In it we live and breathe and are constantly immersed. Were our lungs to cease taking in and pumping out this air, or our bodies relieved of its pressure, we should die.

Small as our globe seems in the light of astronomy, it is not really of the whole globe that we are tenants, but only a part of its surface. In round numbers the globe is 8000 miles in diameter. Thus the skin of the thinnest-skinned apple gives no idea of the relative thinness of the zone of perpendicular distance to which man is confined. And three-fourths of the surface of the globe is covered by water, on which, though man may pass, he cannot dwell; and considerable parts of what remain are made inaccessible by ice. Like a bridge of hair is the line of temperature that we must keep. Investigators tell us of the existence of temperatures of thousands of degrees above zero and thousands of degrees below zero. But man's body must maintain the constant level of a fraction over 98 degrees above zero. A rise or fall of seven degrees either way from this level will kill him. With the permanent rise or fall of a few more degrees in the mean temperature of the surface of the globe it would become uninhabitable by us.

And while all about us, even what seems firmest, is in constant change and motion, so is it with ourselves. These bodies of ours are in reality like the flame of the gas-burner, which has continuous and defined form, but only as a manifestation of changes in the stream of succeeding particles, and which disappears the moment that stream is cut off. What there is real and distinctive in us is that to which we may give a name but cannot explain or easily define — that which gives to changing matter and passing motion the face and form of man.

In all this, man resembles the other animals that with him tenant the superficies of the same earth. Physically he is merely such an animal. Were man only an animal he would be but an inferior animal. Had he no power of providing himself with artificial clothing, man could not exist in many of the regions he now inhabits. He could live only in the most genial and equable parts of the globe.

But man is more than an animal. Though in physical equipment he may in nothing surpass, and in some things fall below other animals, in mental equipment he is so vastly superior as to take him out of their class, and to make him the lord and master of them all. And what more clearly perhaps indicates the deep gulf which separates him from all other animals is that he alone out of all animals is the producer, or bringer forth, and is in that sense the maker. This is a difference which renders the distinction between the highest animal and the lowest man one not of degree but of kind, and which, linked with the animals though he be, justifies the declaration of Scripture that man is created in the likeness of the All-Maker. We know of no race of man so low that they do not raise fruits or vegetables, or domesticate and breed animals; that do not cook foods; that do not fashion weapons; that do not construct habitations; that do not make for themselves garments; that do not adorn themselves or their belongings with ornamentation; that do not draw, paint, sculpt or make music. No animal save man ever kindled a fire or cooked a meal, or made a tool or fashioned a weapon.

It is true that squirrels hide nuts; that birds build nests; that beavers dam streams; that bees construct homes, in which they store the honeyed extract from flowers. But in all this there is nothing akin to the faculties which in these things man displays. What man does, he does by taking thought, by consciously adjusting means to ends. He does it by adapting and contriving and experimenting and copying; by effort after effort and trial after trial

Nature provides for all living things beneath man by implanting in them blind strong impulses which at proper times and seasons prompt them to do what it is necessary they should do. But to man she grants only such impellings of instinct as that which prompts the mother to press the newborn baby to her breast and the baby to suckle. With exceptions such as these, she withdraws from man her guiding power and leaves him to himself. For in him a higher power has arisen and looks out on the world — the power of producing, of making, of causing things to be; a power that seeks to look back into the past ere the globe was, and to peer into a future when it will cease to exist; a power that looks on nature's show with curiosity like that with which an apprentice might scan the master's work, and will ask why tides run and winds blow, and how suns and stars have been put together.

Endowed with reason, and then deprived, or all but deprived, of instinct, man differs from other animals in being the producer. Like them, for instance, he requires food. But while the animals get their food by taking what they find, and are thus limited by what they find already in existence, man has a power of getting his food by bringing it into existence. And so it is with the fulfillment of all his wants; the satisfaction of all his desires. By the use of his animal powers, man can cover perhaps as much ground in a day as can a horse or a dog; he can cross perhaps about as wide a stream. But by virtue of the power that makes him the producer he is already spanning continents and oceans with a speed, a certainty and an ease that not even the birds of most powerful wing can rival.

As this power, which we call reason, rises in man, nature withdraws the light of instinct and leaves him to his own devices — to rise or fall, to soar above the brute or to sink lower. For as the Hebrew Scriptures have phrased it, his eyes are opened and before him are good and evil. The ability to fall, no less than the ability to rise — the very failures and mistakes and perversities of man — show his place and powers. There is among the brutes no drunkenness, no unnatural vice, no waste of effort in accomplishing injurious results, no wanton slaughter of their own kind, no want amid plenty.

Chapter 2 — The Greater Leviathan

Man, as we have any knowledge of him, either in the present or in the past, is always man; differing from other animals in the same way, feeling the same essential needs, moved by the same essential desires, and possessed of the same essential powers.

Yet in tools and weapons; in ease of movement in the transportation; in medicine and surgery; in music in the representative arts; in the extent and precision of the knowledge at his service — the man who is free to the advantages of the civilization of today is as a being of higher order compared to the man whose horizon was bounded, as to the past by a tribal tradition, and as to the present by the mountains or seashore of his immediate home.

But if we analyze the way in which these extensions of man's power of getting and making and knowing and doing are gained, we shall see that they come not from changes in the individual man but from the union of individual powers. There is nothing whatever to show that the men who today build and navigate the steamships that cross the Atlantic at a rate of over five hundred miles a day are one whit superior in any physical or mental quality to their ancestors, whose best vessel was a coracle of wicker and hide. The enormous improvement which these ships show is not an improvement of human nature — it is due to a wider, fuller union of individual efforts in the accomplishment of common ends.

To consider in like manner any one of the many and great advances which civilized man in our time has made is to see that it could only have been gained by the widening cooperation of individual effort. At best, man's individual powers are small and his life is short. What advances would be possible if men were isolated from each other and one generation separated from the next as are the generations of the seventeen-year locusts? The little such individuals might gain during their own lives would be lost with them. Each generation would have to begin from the starting-place of its predecessor.

But man is more than an individual. He is also a social animal, formed and adapted to live and to cooperate with his fellows. It is in this line of social development that the great increase of man's knowledge and powers takes place. The slowness with which we attain the ability to care for ourselves and the qualities incident to our higher gifts involve an overlapping of individuals that continues and extends the family relation beyond the limits which obtain among other mammals. And, beyond this relation, common needs, similar perceptions and like desires, acting among creatures endowed with reason and developing speech, lead to a cooperation of effort that even in its crudest forms gives to man powers that place him far above the beasts and tends to weld individual man into a social body, a larger entity, which has a life and character of its own.

It is in this social body, this larger entity, of which individuals are the atoms, that the extensions of human power which marked the advance of civilization are secured. The rise of civilization is the growth of this cooperation and the increase of the body of knowledge thus obtained and garnered. Perhaps I can better point out what I mean by an illustration:

The famous treatise in which the English philosopher Hobbes, during the revolt against the tyranny of the Stuarts in the seventeenth century, sought to give the sanction of reason to the doctrine of the absolute authority of kings, is titled *Leviathan.* It thus begins:

> *Nature, the art whereby God has made and governs the world, is by the art of man, as in many other things, so in this also imitated, that it can make an artificial animal... for by art is*

> *created the great Leviathan called the Commonwealth or state, and Latin* civitas, *which is but an artificial man; though of greater stature and strength and the natural, for whose protection and defense it was intended; and in which the sovereignty is an artificial soul, as giving life and motion to the whole body; the magistrates and other officers of judicature and execution, artificial joints; reward and punishment, by which fastened to the seat of the sovereignty every joint and member is moved to perform his duty, by the nerves, that do the same in the body natural; the wealth and riches of all the popular members are in the strength;* salus populi, *the people's safety, its business; and counselors by whom all things needful for it to know are suggested onto it, are the memory; equity and laws, an artificial reason and will; concord, health; sedition, sickness; and civil war, death. Lastly, the pacts and covenants, by which the parts of this body politic were at first made, set together, and united, resemble that fiat, or the "let us make man," pronounced by God in the creation.*

Without stopping now to comment further on Hobbes's suggested analogy, there is, it seems to me, in the system or arrangement into which men are brought in social life, by the effort to satisfy their material desires — an integration which goes on as civilization advances — something which even more strongly and more clearly suggests the idea of a gigantic man, formed by the union of individual men, than any merely political integration.

This Greater Leviathan is to the political structure or conscious commonwealth what the unconscious functions of the body are to the conscious activities. It is not made by pacts and covenants, it grows; as the tree grows, as the man himself grows, by virtue of natural laws inherent in human nature and in the constitution of things; and the laws which it in turn obeys, though their manifestations may be retarded or prevented by political action are themselves utterly independent of it, and take no note whatever of political divisions.

This natural system or arrangement, this adjustment of means to ends, of the parts to the whole and the whole to the parts, in the satisfaction of the material desires of man living in society, we call political economy. It is as human units, individuals or families, take their place as integers of this higher man, this Greater Leviathan, that what we call civilization begins and advances.

Chapter 3 — The Meaning of Civilization

The word civilization comes from the Latin *civis*, a citizen. Its original meaning is, the matter or condition in which men live together as citizens. Now the relations of the citizen to other citizens, which are in their conception peaceable and friendly, involving mutual obligations, mutual rights and mutual services, spring from the relation of each citizen to a whole of which each is an integral part. That whole, from membership in which proceeds a relationship of citizens to each other, is the body politic, or political community, which we name the state, and which, struck by the analogy between it and the human body, Hobbes likened to a larger and stronger man made up by the integration of individual men, and called Leviathan.

Yet it is not this political relation, but a relation like it, that is suggested in this word civilization — a relation deeper, wider and closer than the relation of the citizen to the state, and prior to it.

There is a relation between what we call a civilization and what we call a state, but in this civilization is the antecedent and the state is the subsequent. The appearance and development of the body politic, the organized state, is the mark of civilization already in existence. And in the same way the character of the state, the nature of the laws and institutions which it enacts and enforces, indicate the character of the underlying civilization. For while civilization is a general condition, we recognize individual differences in the characteristics of civilization. We speak of ancient civilization and modern civilization; of Asiatic civilization and European civilization; of the Egyptian, the Assyrian, the Chinese civilizations, as separate things, having such general likeness to each other as men have to men, but each marked by such individual characteristics that distinguish one man from other men.

And whether we consider them in their grand divisions or in their minor divisions, the line between what we call civilizations is not the line of separation between bodies politic. The United States and Canada are separate bodies politic, yet their civilization is the same. The making of the Queen of Great Britain Empress of India does not substitute the English civilization for the Indian civilization in Bengal, nor the Indian civilization for the English civilization in Yorkshire or Kent. Change in allegiance involves change in citizenship, but in itself involves no change in the civilization. The civilization is evidently a relation which underlies the relations of the body politic as the unconscious motions of the body underlie the conscious motions.

It is this body economic, or body industrial, which grows up in the cooperation of men to supply their wants and satisfy their desires, that is the real thing constituting what we call civilization. This body economic, or Greater Leviathan, always precedes and always underlies the body politic or Leviathan. The body politic or state is really an outgrowth of the body economic, in fact one of its organs, the need for which and appearance of which arises from and with its own appearance and growth. And from this relation of dependence upon the body economic, the body politic can never become exempt.

Why, then, it may be asked, is it that we take for the greater and precedent a word drawn from the lesser and subsequent, and find in the word civilization, which expresses an analogy to the body politic, the word that serves us as a name for the body economic? The reason of this is worth noting, as it flows from an important principle in the growth of human knowledge. Things that come first in the natural order are not always first apprehended. As the human eye looks out, but not in, so the human mind as it scans the world is apt to observe what is of the superstructure of things before it observes what is of the foundation.

The body politic is more obvious to our eyes, and, so to speak, makes more noise in our ears, than the unseen and silent body economic, from which it proceeds and on which it depends. Thus, in the intellectual development of mankind, it and its relations are noticed sooner and receive names earlier than the body economic. But without at present pursuing further that record of the history of thought that lies in the meaning of words, let us endeavor to see whence comes the integration of man into a body economic and how it grows.

Chapter 4 — The Origin and Genesis of Civilization

Whoever will take the trouble (and if he has the time, he will find in it pleasure) to get on friendly and intimate terms with a dog, a cat, a horse or pig, will find many things in which our "poor relations" resemble us, or perhaps rather, we resemble them.

These animals will exhibit traces at least of all human feelings — love and hate, hope and fear, pride and shame, desire and remorse, vanity and curiosity, generosity and cupidity. Even something of our small vices and acquired tastes they may show. Goats that chew tobacco and like their dram are known on shipboard, and dogs that enjoy carriage-rides and like to run to fires, on land. I bought in Calcutta, when a boy, a monkey which all the long way home would pillow her head on mine as I slept, and keep off my face the cockroaches that infested the old Indiaman by catching them with her hands and cramming them into her maw. When I got home, she was so jealous of a little brother that I had to part with her to a lady who had no children. And my own children had in New York a little monkey, sent them from Paraguay, that so endeared herself to us all that when she died from over-indulgence in needle-points and pin-heads it seemed like losing a member of the family. She knew my step before I reached the door on coming home, and when it opened would spring to meet me with chattering caresses, the more prolonged the longer I had been away. She leaped from the shoulder of one to that of another at table; nicely discriminating between those who had been good to her and those who had offended her. At the time for school-children to pass by, she would perch before a front window and cut monkey shines for their amusement, chattering with delight at their laughter and applause, as she sprang from curtain to curtain and showed the convenience of a tail that one may swing by.

One of the most striking differences between man and the lower animals is that which distinguishes man as the unsatisfied animal. Yet I am not sure that this is in itself an original difference; an essential difference of kind. I am, on the contrary, as I come to consider it, inclined rather to think it a result of the endowment of man with the quality of reason that animals lack, than in itself an original difference.

For we see that, to some extent at least, the desires of animals increase as opportunities for gratifying them are afforded. Give a horse lump-sugar and he will come to you again to get it, though in his natural state he aspires to nothing beyond the herbage. The pampered lap-dogs whose tails stick out from warm clothes on the fashionable city avenues in winter seem to enjoy their clothing, though they could never solve the mystery of how to put it on, let alone how to make it. Even man is content with the best he can get until he begins to see he can get better. A handsome woman I have met, who puts on for a ball or opera an earl's ransom in gems, and must have a cockade in her coachman's hat and bicycle tires on her carriage wheels, will tell you that once her greatest desire was for a new wash-tub and a better cooking-stove.

The more we come to know the animals the harder we find it to draw any clear mental line between them and us, except on one point, as to which we may see a clear and profound distinction. This, that animals lack and that men have, is the power of tracing effect to cause, and from cause assuming effect.

Is it not in this power of "thinking things out," of "seeing the way through" — the power of tracing causal relations — that we find the essence of what we call reason, the possession of which constitutes the unmistakable difference, not in degree but in kind, between man and brutes, and enables him, though their fellow on the plane of material existence, to assume mastery and lordship over them all?

Here is the germ of civilization. It is this power of relating effect to cause and cause to effect which renders the world intelligible to man; which enables him to understand the connection of things around him and the bearings of things above and beyond him; to live not merely in the present, but to pry into the past and to forecast the future; to distinguish not only what are presented to him through the senses, but things of which the senses cannot tell; to recognize as through mists a power from which the world itself and all that exists therein must have proceeded; to know that he himself shall surely die, but to believe that after that he shall live again.

Gifted alone with the power of relating cause and effect, man is among all animals the only producer in the true sense of the term. He is a producer, even in the savage state; and would endeavor to produce even in a world where there was no other man. But the same quality of reason which makes him the producer, also, where ever exchange becomes possible, makes him the exchanger. And it is along this line of exchanging that the body economic is evolved and develops, and that all the advances of civilization are primarily made.

But the first human pair to appear in the world could not have begun to use the higher forms of that power until their numbers had increased. With this increase of numbers the cooperation of efforts in the satisfaction of desires would begin. Aided at first by the natural affections, it would be carried beyond that point by that quality of reason which enables a man to see what the animal cannot, that by parting with what is less desired in exchange for what is more desired, a net increase in satisfaction is obtained.

With the beginning of exchange or trade among man this body economic begins to form, and in its beginning civilization begins. As trade begins in different places and proceeds from different centers, sending out the network of exchange which relates men to each other through their needs and desires, different bodies economic begin to form and to grow in different places, each with distinguishing characteristics which, like the characteristics of the individual face and voice, are so fine as only to be appreciated relatively, and are better recognized than expressed.

We are accustomed to speak of certain peoples as uncivilized, and of certain other peoples as civilized or fully civilized, but in truth such use of terms is merely relative. To find an utterly uncivilized people we must find a people among whom there is no exchange or trade. Such a people does not exist, and, so far as our knowledge goes, never did. To find a fully civilized people we must find a people among whom exchange or trade is absolutely free and has reached the fullest development to which human desires can carry it. There is, as yet, unfortunately, no such people.

Chapter 5 — Knowledge and Skill

In contrasting man in the civilized state with man in his primitive state I have dwelt most on the gain in the power of gratifying material desires, because such gains are the most obvious. Yet as thoughts precede action, the essential gain which these indicate must be in knowledge. That the ocean steamship takes the place of the hollow log, the great modern building of the rude hut, shows a larger knowledge utilized in such constructions.

To consider the nature of this gain in knowledge is to see that it is not due to improvement in the individual power of knowing, but to the larger and wider cooperation of individual powers; to the growth of that body of knowledge which is a part, or rather, perhaps, an aspect of the social integration I have called the body economic. If we could separate the individuals whose knowledge, correlated and combined, is expressed in the ocean steamship or great modern building, it is doubtful if their separate knowledge would suffice for more than the constructions and tools of the savage.

The knowledge that comes closest to the individual is what we call skill. Whoever, in mature years, has learned to do some new thing, as for instance to ride a bicycle, knows how slowly and painfully such knowledge is acquired. At first each leg and foot, each arm and hand, seems to need separate direction, which the conscious mind cannot give so quickly and in such order as to prevent the learner from running into what he would avoid. But as the effort is continued, the knowledge of how to direct these muscles passes from the domain of the conscious to that of the subconscious mind, and the needed correction takes place automatically. With continued effort, the knowledge required for the proper movement of the muscles becomes so fully stored in the subconscious memory that at length the learner may ride easily, indulging in other trains of thought and noticing persons and scenery. His hard-gotten knowledge has passed into skill.

Now, because skill is that part of knowledge which comes closest to the individual, becoming as it were a part of his being, it is the knowledge which is longest retained, and is also that which cannot be communicated from one to another, or so communicated only in very small degree. You may give a man general directions as to how to ride a bicycle or operate a typewriter, but he can get the skill necessary to do either only by practice.

As to this part of knowledge at least, it is clear that the advances of civilization do not imply any gain in the power of the individual to acquire knowledge. Not only do antiquities show that in the arts then cultivated the men of thousands of years ago were as skillful as the man of today, but we see the same thing in our contact with people whom we deem the veriest savages. The Australian black fellow will throw a boomerang in a way that excites the wonder of the civilized man. On the other hand, the European with sufficient practice will learn to handle the boomerang or practice any of the other arts of the savages as skillfully as they, and wild tribes to whom the horse and firearms are first introduced by Europeans become excellent riders and most expert marksmen.

It is not in skill, but in the knowledge which can be communicated from one to another, that the civilized man shows his superiority to the savage. This knowledge, since it is not concerned with the government of the organs directly responsive to the conscious will, does not come as close to the individual as skill, but is held rather as a possession of the organ of conscious memory, then as a part of the individual himself.

Now, this is the knowledge which constitutes the body of

knowledge that so vastly increases with the progress of civilization. It is transferable by speech; and it becomes capable of more permanent storage and of wider and easier transferability — manuscripts, books, and so on.

This ability to store and transmit knowledge in other and better ways than in the individual memory and in individual speech, which comes with the integration of individual man in the social body or body economic, is of itself an enormous gain in the advance of the sum of knowledge. But the gain in other and allied directions that comes from the larger and closer integration of individuals in the social man is greater still. Of all the systematized knowledges, that which we call astronomy was probably one of the earliest. Consider the first star-gazers, who with no instrument of observation but the naked eye, and no means of record save the memory, sought by watching night after night related movements in heavenly bodies. How little even of their own ability to gather and store knowledge could they apply to the getting of such knowledge. For until civilization had passed its first stages, the knowledge and skill required to satisfy their own material needs must have very seriously lessened the energy that could be applied to the gaining of any other knowledge.

Compare with such an observer of the stars, the stargazer who watches now in one of the great modern observatories. Consider the long vistas of knowledge and skill, of experiment and meditation and effort, that are involved in the existence of the building itself, with its mechanical devices; in the great lenses; in the ponderous tube so easily adjusted; and the delicate instruments for measuring time and space and temperature; in the tables of logarithms and mechanical means for affecting calculations; in the lists of recorded observations and celestial atlases that may be consulted; in the means of communicating by telegraph and telephone with other observers in other places, that now characterize a well-appointed observatory, and in the means and appliances for securing the comfort and freedom from distraction of the observer himself! To consider all these is to begin to realize how much the cooperation of other men contributes to the work of even such a specialized individual as he who watches the stars.

Chapter 6 — Natural Laws

In the phenomena presented to him, man must early notice two kinds of relation. Some things show themselves with other things, and some things follow other things. These two kinds of relation we call relations of coexistence and relations of succession or sequence. Since what continues is not so apt to attract our attention as what changes, it is probable that the first of these two relations to be noticed is that of succession. Light comes with the appearance of luminous bodies of the firmament, and darkness with their disappearance. Night succeeds day, and day night; spring the winter, and summer the spring; the leaf, the bud; and wind and rain the heavy threatening cloud.

But to note the relation of things in succession does not content man. The essential quality of reason leads him to ask why one thing follows another, and in the relation of sequence to assume or to seek for a relation of con-sequence.

Let us fix in our minds the meaning of these two words. For even by usually careful writers one of them is sometimes used when the other is really meant, which brings about confusion of thought where precision is needed.

The meaning of sequence is that which follows or succeeds. The meaning of consequence is that which follows from. To say that one thing is a consequence of another, is to say that one has to the other a relation not merely of succession, but of necessary succession, the relation namely of effect to cause.

Now of the sequences which we notice in external nature, some are variable, that is to say, they do not always follow what is given as the antecedent, while some are invariable, that is to say, they always follow what is given as the antecedent. As to these invariable sequences, which we properly call consequences, we give a name to the causal connection between what we apprehend as effect and what we assume as cause by calling it a law of nature. What we mean by this term is a matter too important to be left in the uncertainty and confusion with which it is treated in the standard economic works. Let us therefore, before beginning to use the term, try to discover how it has come into use, that we may fully understand it.

When, proceeding from what we apprehend as effect or consequence, we begin to seek cause, it in most cases happens that the first cause we find, as accounting for the phenomena, we soon come to see to be in itself an effect or consequence of an antecedent which to it is cause. Thus our search for cause begins again, leading us from one link to another link in the chain of causation, until we come to a cause which we can apprehend as capable of setting in motion the series of which the particular result is the effect or consequence.

Now the only way in which we can hope to discover what to us is yet unknown is by reasoning to it from what to us is known. What we know most directly and immediately is that in us which feels and wills; that which to distinguish from our own organs, parts or powers we call the ego, or I; that which distinguishes us, ourselves, from the external world. That which really distinguishes man from external nature; that which seems to come into the world with the dawning of life and to depart from it with the death, is that whose identity I recognize as "me," through all changes of matter and motion. It is this which not only receives the impressions brought to it through the senses, but by the use of the power we call imagination contemplates itself, as one may look at his own face in a mirror. In this way the ego or I of man may reason, not only upon the phenomena of the external world as presented to it through the senses, but also its own nature, its own powers, and its own activities, and regard the world, external and internal, as a whole, having for its components not merely matter and energy, but also spirit.

The simplest causal relation we perceive is that which we find in our own consciousness. I scratch my head, I slap my leg, and feel the effects. I drink, and my thirst is quenched. Here we have perhaps the closest connection between consequence and cause. Passing beyond the point where both cause and effect are known by consciousness, we carry the certainty thus derived to the explanation of phenomena as to which cause and effect, one or both, lie beyond consciousness. I throw a stone at a bird and it falls. This result, the fall of the bird, is made known to me indirectly through my sense of sight, and later when I pick it up, by my sense of touch. The bird falls because the stone hit it. The stone hit it because put in motion by the movement of my hand and arm. And the movement of my hand and arm was because of my exertion of will, known to me directly by consciousness.

What we apprehend as the beginning cause in any series, whether we call it primary cause or final cause, is always to us *the* cause or sufficient reason of the particular result. And this point in causation at which we rest satisfied is that which implies the element of spirit, the exertion of will. For it is of the nature of human reason never to rest content until it can come to something that may be conceived of as acting in itself, and not merely as a consequence of something else as antecedent, and thus be taken as the cause of the results or consequence from which the backward search began. Thus, in our instance, leaving out intermediate links in the chain of causation, and proceeding at once from results to ultimate cause, or sufficient reason, we say correctly that the bird fell because I hit it — that is, because I exerted in an effective way the will to hit it.

But I know, by consciousness, that in me the exertion of will proceeds from some motive or desire. And reasoning from what I know to explain what I wish to discover, I explain similar acts and others by similar desires.

How early and how strong is the disposition to seek cause in exertion of will prompted by desire is shown in the prattle of children, and the folk-lore and fairy tales. We are at first apt to attribute even to what we afterwards learn are inanimate things the exertion of will and the promptings of desire such as we find in our own consciousness, and to say, not as figures of speech, but as recognitions of cause, that the sun smiles and the clouds threaten and the wind blows for this or that purpose or with this or that intent.

And in the earliest of such recognitions we find the moral element, which belongs alone to spirit. What mother has not soothed her child by threatening or pretending to whip the naughty chair or bad stone that caused her little girl or boy to stumble, and has not held the little thing in rapt silence with stories of talking animals and thinking trees? But as we look closer, we see that the power of reason is not in animals, nor volition in sticks and stones. Yet still seeking cause behind effect, and not satisfied that we have found cause until we have come to spirit, we find rest for awhile by accounting for effects that we cannot trace to will in man or animals, on the assumption of will in supersensible forms, and thus gratify the longing of the reason to discover cause, by peopling rivers and mountains and lakes and seas and trees and seasons with spirits and genii, and fairies and goblins, and angels and devils, and special gods.

Yet, in and through this stage of human thought grows the apprehension of an order and co-relation in things, which we can understand only by assuming unity of will and comprehensiveness of intent — of an all-embracing system or order which we personify as Nature, and of a great "I am" from whose exertion of will all things visible and invisible proceed, and which is the first or all-beginning cause. In every direction the effort of the reason to seek the cause of what it perceives, forces this upon the thoughtful mind.

The things that show most clearly the adaptation of means to ends, so that we can at once understand their genesis and divide their cause, are things made by man, such as houses, clothing, tools, and ornaments, machines; in short, what we call human productions. These, as evincing the adaptation of means to ends, have an unmistakable character. The coming upon a piece of clothing, or a brooch or ring, or tomahawk or bow, or the embers and fragments of a cooked meal, would have been as quick and even surer proof of the presence of man on his supposed desert island than were to Robinson Crusoe the footprints in the sand. For of all the beings that our senses give us knowledge of, man is the only one that in himself has the power of adapting means to ends by taking thought. Yet, so soon as man looks out, he finds in the world itself evidences of the same power of adapting means to ends that characterize his own works. Hence, recognizing in the sum of perceptible things — exclusive of himself, or rather of his essential principal or ego, but inclusive, not merely of his bodily, but also of his mental frame — a system or whole, composed of related parts, he personifies it in thought and calls it Nature.

We frequently use the word nature to avoid the necessity of naming that which we feel to be unnameable, in the sense of being beyond our comprehension, and therefore beyond our power of defining. Yet I think that not merely the almost universal, but the clearest and therefore best, perceptions of mankind, really distinguish what we call Nature from what we call God, just as we distinguish the ship, or other machine, that we personify, from the will which we recognize as exerted in its origination and being; and that at the bottom our idea is that of Pope:

All are but parts of one stupendous whole,
Whose body nature is, and God the soul.

It is from this conception of Nature as expressing or as animated by the highest will, that we derive, I think, the term "law of Nature." Whatever we observe as an invariable relation of things, of which in the last analysis we can affirm only that "it is always so," we call a law of Nature. But though we use this phrase to express the fact of invariable relation, something more than this is suggested. The term itself involves the idea of a causative will. As John Stuart Mill, trained to analysis from infancy, and from infancy exempt from theological bias, says:

> *The expression "law of Nature" is generally employed by scientific man with a sort of tacit reference to the original sense of the word law, namely, the expression of the will of the superior – the superior, in this instance, being the Ruler of the universe.*

Thus, when we find in Nature certain invariable sequences, whose cause of being transcends the power of the will testified to by our own consciousness — such, for instance, as that stones and apples always fall towards the earth; that the square of a hypotenuse is always equal to the sum of the squares of its base and perpendicular; that gases always coalesce in certain definite proportions; that one pole of the magnet always attracts what the other always repels; that at a certain stage of infancy teeth appear, and later decay and drop out; and so on through the list of invariable sequences that these will suggest — we say, for it is really all that we can say, that these sequences are invariable because they belong to the order or system of Nature; or, in short, that they are "laws of Nature."

The dog and cow sometimes look wise enough to be meditating. If they really could bother their heads with such matters or express their ideas in speech, they would probably say that such sequences are invariable, and then rest. But a man is impelled by his endowment of reason to seek behind fact for cause. Thus, whether civilized or uncivilized, man is compelled to look for cause beneath the phenomena that he begins really to consider, and no matter what intermediate cause he may find, cannot be content until he reaches will and finds or assumes intent. This necessity is universal to human nature, for it belongs to that quality or principle of reason which essentially distinguishes man from the brute.

Beneath the belief of the savage in totems and amulets and charms and witchcraft works the recognition of spirit; and the philosophies that have hardened into grotesque forms of religion contain at bottom that idea of an originating will which the Hebrew Scriptures express in their opening sentence: "In the beginning God created the heaven and the earth."

To such recognition of will or spirit, reason, as it searches from effect for cause, must come before it can rest content. Beyond this, reason cannot go. Why is it that some things always coexist with other things? and that some things always follow other things? The Mohammedan will answer: "it is the will of God." The man of our Western civilization will answer: "it is a law of Nature." The phrase is different, but the answer one.

Chapter 7 — The Knowledge Properly Called Science

Science is a word much abused just now, when all sorts of pretenders to special knowledge style themselves scientists, and all sorts of ill-verified speculations are called sciences; yet it has a well-defined, proper meaning which may easily be kept in mind. In its proper and definite meaning, science is that knowledge by or in which phenomena are related to what we assume to be their cause, and called a law or laws of nature.

With human laws what is properly called science has nothing whatever to do, unless it be as phenomena which it subjects to examination in the effort to discover in natural law their cause. Thus there may be a science of jurisprudence, or a science of legislation, as there may be a science of grammar, a science of language, or a science of the mental structure and its operations. But the object of such sciences, properly so-called, is always to discover the laws of nature in which human laws, customs and modes of thought originate — the natural laws which lie behind and permanently affect, not nearly all external manifestations of human will, but even the internal affections of that will itself.

Human laws are made by man, and share in all his weaknesses and frailties. They must be enforced by penalties subsequent to and conditioned upon their violation. Unless accompanied by some penalty for its violation, no act of legislative body or sovereign prince becomes law. Human laws are acknowledged only by man; and that not by all men in all times and places, but only by some men — that is, by men living in the time and place where the political power that imposes them has the ability to enforce their sanctions; and not even by all of these men, but generally by only a very small part of them. Limited to the circumscribed areas which we call political divisions, they are even there constantly fluctuating and changing.

Natural laws, on the other hand, belong to the natural order of things. They have no sanctions in the sense of penalties imposed upon their violation, and enforced subsequent to their violation; they cannot be violated. Man can no more resist or swerve natural law than he can build the world. Their sway extends not merely over and throughout the whole earth of which we are constantly changing tenants, but over and through the whole system of which it is a part, and so far as either observation or reason can give us light, over and through the whole universe.

I dwell again on the distinction between laws of nature and laws of man, because it is necessary, in beginning the study of political economy, that we should grasp it firmly and keep it clearly in mind. This necessity is the greater, since we shall find that in the accredited economic treatises laws of nature and laws of man are confused together in what they call laws of political economy.

It is not worthwhile to make many quotations to show a confusion which one may see by taking up the economic work approved by college or university that first comes to his hand; but that what passes in these institutions for the science of political economy may speak for itself, I shall make one quotation.

I take for that purpose the best book I can find that puts into compact form the teachings of the scholastic economists. It is the *Primer of Political Economy in Sixteen Definitions and Forty Propositions* by Mason and Lalor. Their primer has been widely endorsed and largely used in institutions of learning. In this is the first of their sixteen definitions, and their explanation of it:

> *DEFINITION I. – Political Economy is the Science which teaches the laws that regulate the Production, Distribution and Exchange of Wealth.*
>
> *Everything in this world is governed by law. Human laws are those made by man. All others are natural laws. A law providing*

for the education of children in schools is a human law. The law that children shall keep growing, if they live, until they are men and women, and shall then slowly decay and at last die, is a natural law. An apple falls from a tree and the earth moves around the sun in obedience to natural laws. The laws which regulate the production, distribution and exchange of wealth are of both kinds. The more important ones, however, are natural.

In this Messrs. Mason and Lalor aptly illustrate the essential difference between natural law and human law. But the way in which the two are mixed together as economic laws suggests the examination-paper of the Philadelphia boy more interested in hooking catfish and stoning frogs than in his lessons. To the question, "Name and describe nouns?" the answer was:

> *Nouns are three in number and sometimes more. There are proper nouns, common nouns, bloody nouns* and other nouns. Proper nouns are the properest nouns, but common nouns are the commonest. Bloody nouns are the big ones. Other nouns are no good.*

Yet ridiculous as is this confusion of human law and natural law, and absurd as is a definition that leaves one to guess what is meant by "laws," this little primer correctly gives what is to be found in the pretentious treatises it endeavors to condense.

It is only with the implication that by law is meant natural law, that we can say "Everything in this world is governed by law." To say, as the little summary of the scholastic political economy from which I have quoted says, that political economy is the science which teaches the laws, some of them natural laws and some of them human laws, which regulate the production, distribution and exchange of wealth, is like saying that astronomy is a science

*A name given by boys in Philadelphia to large bullfrogs.

which teaches the laws, some of them laws of matter and motion and some of them Bulls of Popes and Acts of Parliament, which regulate the movements of stars and comets.

The absurdity of this is not so strikingly obvious in the ponderous treatises from which it is derived as in this little primer, because their reader's attention is confused by their utter lack of logical arrangement, and distracted by the shoveling in on him, as it were, of great masses of irrelevant matter, which makes it a most difficult task to dig out what is really meant — a task usually abandoned by the ordinary reader with a secret feeling of shame at his own incapacity to follow such deep and learned men. The expositions of what passes for the science of political economy in our schools do indeed for the most part contain some things that really belong to science. But in their larger part what properly belongs to science is, in the literature of political economy that has grown up since his time, confused and overlaid with what Turgot, over a hundred years ago, spoke of as an art — the art, namely, "of those who set themselves to darken things that are clear to the open mind."

What this truly great Frenchman of the eighteenth century said is worth quoting, For it finds abundant and constant illustration in the writings of the professors of political economy of the nineteenth century, and especially in the latest of them:

> *This art consists in never beginning at the beginning, but in rushing into the subject in all its complications, or with some fact that is only an exception, or some circumstance, isolated, far-fetched or merely collateral, which does not belong to the essence of the question and goes for nothing in its solution.... Like a geometer who treating of triangles should begin with white triangles as most simple, in order to treat afterwards of blue triangles, then of red triangles, and so on.*

If political economy is a science — and if not it is hardly worth the while of earnest men to bother themselves with it — it must follow the rules of science, and seek in natural law the causes of the phenomena which it investigates. With human law, except as furnishing illustrations and supplying subjects for its investigation, it has, as I have already said, nothing whatever to do. It is concerned with the permanent, not with the transient; with the laws of nature, not with the laws of man.

Chapter 8 — The Meaning and Scope of Political Economy

Adam Smith, who at the close of the last century gave so powerful impulse to the study of what has since been called political economy that he is, not without justice, spoken of as its father, entitled his great book *An Inquiry into the Nature and Causes of the Wealth of Nations,* and what we call political economy, the Germans call national economy.

No term is of importance if we rightly understand what it means. But, both in the term "political economy," and in that of "national economy," as well as in the phrase "wealth of nations," lurk suggestions which may and in fact often do interfere with a clear apprehension of the ground they properly cover. The use of the term "political economy" began at a time when the distinction between natural law and human law was not clearly made, when what I have called the body economic was largely confounded with what is properly the body politic, and when it was the common opinion in Europe, even of thoughtful men, that the production and distribution of wealth were to be regulated by the legislative action of the sovereign or state.

The term was given currency by those French exponents of natural right, or the natural order, who today may be best described as the first single-tax men. They used the term "political economy" to distinguish from politics the branch of knowledge with which they were concerned, and from this called themselves Economists. The term is used by Adam Smith only in speaking of "this sect," composed of "a few men of great learning and ingenuity in France." But although these Economists were overwhelmed and have been almost forgotten, yet of their "noble and generous system" this term remained, and since the time of Adam Smith it has come into general use as expressive of — to accept the most common and I think sufficient definition — that branch of knowledge that treats of the nature of wealth, and the laws of its production and distribution.

It is not with the body politic, but with that body social or body industrial that I have called the body economic, that political economy is directly concerned; not with the commonwealth of which man becomes a member by the attribution or acceptance of allegiance to a republic; but with the commonwealth of which he becomes a member by the fact that he lives in the state of society in which each does not attempt to satisfy all of his own material needs by his own direct efforts, but obtains the satisfaction of some of them at least through the cooperation of others. The fact of participation in this cooperation does not make him a citizen of any particular state. It makes him a civilized man, a member of the civilized world — a unit in that body economic to which political distinctions of states and nations have no more relation than distinctions of color have to distinctions of form.

An economy of the economic unit would not be a political economy, and the laws of which it would treat would not be those with which political economy is concerned. They would be the laws of personal or family conduct. An economy of the individual or family could treat the production of wealth no further than related to the production of such a unit. And though it might take cognizance of the physical laws involved in its agriculture and mechanics, of the distribution of wealth in the economic sense it could not treat at all, since any apportionment among the members of such a family of wealth obtained by it would be governed by the laws of individual or family life, and not by any law of the distribution of the results of socially conjoined effort.

But when in the natural course of human growth and development economic units come into such relations that the satisfaction of material desires is sought by conjoined effort, the laws which political economy seeks to discover begin to appear.

The system or arrangement which is the proper purpose of political economy to discover may be likened to that system or arrangement by which the physical body is nourished. The lowest unit of animal life, so far as we can see, is a single cell, which sucks in and assimilates its own food; thus directly satisfying what we may style its own desires. But in those highest forms of animal life of which man is a type, myriads of cells have become conjoined in related parts and organs, exercising different and complex functions, which results in the procurement, digestion and assimilation of the food that, nourishing each separate cell, maintains the entire organism. Brain and stomach, hands and feet, eyes and ears, teeth and hair, bones, nerves, arteries and veins, still less the cells of which all these parts are composed, do not feed themselves. Under the government of the brain, what the hands, aided by the legs, assisted by the organs of sense, procure, is taken to the mouth, masticated by the teeth, taken by the throat to the alembic of the stomach, where aided by the intestines it is digested, and passing into a fluid containing all nutritive substances, is oxygenized by the lungs; and impelled by the pumping of the heart, makes a complete circuit of the body through a system of arteries and veins, in the course of which every part and every cell takes the nutriment it requires.

Now, what the blood is to the physical body, wealth, as we shall hereafter see more fully, is to the body economic. And as we should find, were we to undertake it, that a description of the manner in which blood is produced and distributed in the physical body would involve almost, if not quite, the description of the entire physical man with all his powers and functions, so we shall find that what is included in political economy is almost, if not quite, the whole body social, with all its parts, powers and functions, and laws under which they operate.

The scope of political economy would be roughly explained were we to style it the science which teaches how civilized men get a living. Why this idea is sufficiently expressed as the production and distribution of wealth will be more fully seen hereafter; but there is a distinction as to what is called getting a living that it may be worthwhile to note here.

We have but to look at existing facts to see that there are two ways in which a man may obtain satisfaction of his material desires for things not freely supplied to him by nature. The first of these ways is, by working, or rendering service. The second is, by stealing, or extorting service.

But there is only one way in which man (i.e., man in general or all men) can satisfy his material desires — that is by working, or rendering service. For it is manifestly impossible that man in general or all men, or indeed any but a small minority of men, can satisfy their material desires by stealing, since in the nature of things working or the rendering of service is the only way in which the material satisfactions of desire can be primarily obtained or produced. Stealing produces nothing; it only alters the distribution of what has already been produced

Therefore, a true science of political economy takes no cognizance of stealing, except in so far as the various forms of it may pervert the natural distribution, and thus check the natural production of wealth.

Nor does political economy concern itself with the character of the desires for which satisfaction is sought. It is, so to speak, like the science of navigation, which is concerned with the means whereby a ship may be carried from point to point on the ocean, but asks not whether that ship may be a pirate or a missionary barque, or what are the expectations which may induce its passengers to go from one place to another. Political economy is not a moral or ethical science, nor yet is it a political science. It is the science of the maintenance and nutriment of the body politic.

Although it will be found incidentally to throw a most powerful light upon, and to give the most powerful support to, the teachings of moral or ethical science, its proper business is neither to explain the difference between right and wrong nor to persuade to one in preference to the other.

Chapter 9 — The Elements of Political Economy

The complex phenomena of the production and distribution of wealth in the elaborate organization of modern civilization will only puzzle us, as the many confused and confusing books written to explain it show, if we began, as it were, from the middle. But if we seek first principles and trace out main lines, so as to comprehend the skeleton of their relation, they will readily become intelligible.

To understand a complex machine the best way is first to see what is the beginning and what the end of its movements, leaving details until we have mastered its general idea and comprehended its purpose. In this way we most easily see the relation of parts to each other and to the subject of the whole.

When the safety bicycle was yet a curiosity even in the towns of England and the United States, an American missionary in a far-off station received from an old friend, unaccompanied by the letter intended to go with it, a present of one of these machines, which for economy in transportation had not been set up, but was forwarded in its unassembled parts. How these parts were to be put together was a perplexing problem, for neither the missionary himself nor anyone he could consult could at first imagine what the thing was intended to do, and their guesses were of almost anything but the truth, until at length the saddle suggested a theory, which was so successfully followed that by the time, months afterwards, another shipment brought the missing letter, the missionary was riding over the hard sand of the beach on his wheel.

The immense aggregate of movements by which, in civilization, wealth is produced and distributed, viewed collectively as the subject of political economy constitute a system or arrangement much greater than, yet analogous to, the system or arrangement of a great factory. In the attempt to understand the laws of nature, which they illustrate and obey, let us avoid the confusion that inevitably attends beginning from the middle, by proceeding in the way suggested in our illustration — the only scientific way.

These movements, so various in their modes, and so complex in their relations, with which political economy is concerned, evidently originate in the exertion of human will, prompted by desire; their means are the material and forces that nature offers to man and the natural laws which these obey; their end and aim the satisfaction of man's material desires. If we try to call to mind as many as we can of the different movements that are included in the production and distribution of wealth in modern civilization — the catching and gathering, the separating and combining, the digging and planting, the baking and brewing, the weaving and dyeing, the sewing and washing, the sawing and planing, the melting and forging, the moving and transporting, the buying and selling — we shall see that what they all aim to accomplish is some sort of change in the place, form or relation of the materials or forces supplied by nature so as to better satisfy human desire.

Thus the movements with which political economy is concerned are human actions, having for their aim the attainment of material satisfactions. And the laws that it is its province to discover are not the laws manifested in the existence of the materials and forces of nature that man thus utilizes, nor yet the laws which make possible their change in place, form or relation, but the laws of man's own nature.

The world, regarded from the standpoint of political economy, has for its original elements, man and nature. Of these, the human element is the initiative or active factor — that which begins or acts first. The natural element is the passive factor — that which receives action and responds to it. From the interaction of these two proceed all with which political economy is concerned.

Between the material things which come into existence through man's agency and those which come into existence through the agency of nature alone, the difference is as clear to human reason as the difference between a mountain and a pyramid. Whatever man makes must have for its substance pre-existing matter; whatever motion he exerts must be drawn from a pre-existing stock of energy. Take away from man all that is contributed by external nature, and you have, what? Something which has no form or substance or direct power in or over the material world, but which is yet the originating impulse which utilizes motion to mold matter into forms it desires — and to which we must look for the origin of the pyramid.

We cannot really consider the beginning of things without seeing that when man came into the world, the sum of energy was not increased, nor that of matter added to — and so it must be today. In all the changes that man brings about in the material world, he adds nothing to and subtracts nothing from the sum of matter and energy. He merely brings about changes in the place and relation of what already exists, and the first and always indispensable condition to his doing anything in the material world, and indeed to his very existence therein, is that of access to its material and forces.

The steam engine rushing along with its long train of coal or goods or passengers is, in all that is evident to our senses, but a new form of what previously existed. Everything about it that we can see, hear, touch, taste, weigh, measure or subject to chemical tests, existed before man was. What has brought pre-existing matter and motion into the shape, place and function of an engine and train is that which, prisoned in the engineer's brain, grasps the throttle;

the same thing that in the infant stretches for the moon, and in the child makes mud-pies. It is this conscious will seeking the gratification of its desires in the alteration of material forms that is the primary motive power, the active factor, in bringing about the relations with which political economy deals. And this will can act only in certain ways, and is subject in that action to certain uniform sequences, which we term laws of nature.

Chapter 10 — The Fundamental Law of Political Economy

Desire is the prompter, and the satisfaction of desire is the end and aim, of all human action. All that men seek to do, to obtain or to avoid may be embraced in one term, as satisfactions of desire. But of these desires and their corresponding satisfactions, some are more primary or fundamental than others; and it is only as these desires obtain satisfaction that other desires arise and are felt. Thus the desire for air is perhaps the most fundamental of all human desires. Yet its satisfaction is under normal conditions so easily had that we usually are not conscious of it — it is in fact rather a latent than an actual desire. But let one be shut off from air, and the desire to get it becomes at once the strongest of desires, casting out for the moment all others. So it is with other desires, such as those for food and drink, the satisfaction of which is necessary to the maintenance of life and health and the avoidance of injury and pain, and which we share in common with the brute. These primary desires lie as it were beneath, or are fundamental to, the manifold desires which arise in man when they are satisfied. For, while the desires of other animals seem comparatively few and fixed, the desires of man are seemingly illimitable. He is indeed the never-satisfied animal, his desires under normal conditions growing with his power of satisfying them without assignable limit.

Now, of human desires and their corresponding satisfactions, some may be subjective, that is, relating to the individual mind or thinking subject; and some objective, that is, relating to the external world, the object of its thought. And by another distinction, some may be said to be immaterial, that is, relating to things not cognizable by the senses, i.e., thought and feelings; and some to be material, that is, relating to things cognizable by the senses, i.e., matter and energy.

In the order of human desires, what we call needs come first, and are of the widest importance. Desires that transcend the desires of the animal can arise and seek gratification only when the desires we share with other animals are satisfied. And those who are inclined to deem that branch of philosophy which is concerned with the gratification of material needs, and especially with the way in which men are fed, clothed and sheltered, as a secondary and ignoble science, are like an architect who should deem the ornamentation of a façade more important than the laying of a foundation.

The only way man has of satisfying his desires is by action.

Now action, if continued long enough in one line to become really exertion, a conscious putting forth of effort, produces in the consciousness a feeling of reluctance or weariness. This comes from something deeper than the exhaustion of energy in what we call physical labor; for whoever has tried it knows that one may lie on his back in the most comfortable position and by mere dint of sustained thinking, without consciously moving a muscle, tire himself as truly as by sawing wood; and that the mere clash and conflict of the involuntary or undirected thought or feeling, or its continuance in one direction, will soon bring extreme weariness.

But whatever be its ultimate cause, the fact is that labor, the attempt of the conscious will to realize its material desire, is always, when continued for a little while, in itself hard and irksome. And whether from this fact alone, or from this fact, conjoined with or based upon something intuitive to our perceptions, the further fact, testified to both by observation of our own feelings and actions and by observation of the acts of others, is that men always seek to gratify their desires with the least exertion.

This, of course, does not mean that they always succeed in doing so, any more than the physical law that motion tends to persist in a straight line means that moving bodies always take that line. But it does mean the mental analogue of the physical law that motion seeks the line of least resistance — that is seeking to gratify their desires men will always seek the way which under existing physical, social and personal conditions seems to them to involve the least expenditure of exertion.

This disposition of man is so universal and unfailing that it constitutes one of those invariable sequences that we denominate laws of nature, and from which we may safely reason. It is this law of nature that is the fundamental law of political economy — the central law from which its deductions and explanations may with certainty be drawn, and, indeed, by which alone they become possible. It holds the same place in the sphere of political economy that the law of gravitation does in physics. Without it there could be no recognition of order, and all would be chaos.

Yet the failure clearly to apprehend this has led to very serious and widespread mistakes as to the nature of the science. For the principle that men always seek to satisfy their desires with the least exertion, there has been substituted the principle of human selfishness. And with the assumption that political economy takes into its account only the selfish feelings of human nature, there have been linked, as laws of political economy, other assumptions as destitute of validity. This presumption, that political economy must eliminate everything but the selfish feelings of mankind, has continued to pervade the accredited political economy up to this time, whatever may have been the effects of the attacks made upon it by those, who, not putting their objections into logical and coherent form, could be spoken of its sentimentalists, but not political economists. Yet, however generally the accepted writers on political economy may have themselves supposed the assumption of universal selfishness to be the fundamental principle of political economy, or how much ground they may have given for such a supposition on the part of their readers, a true political economy requires no such assumption. The primary postulate on and from which its whole structure is built is not that all men are governed only by selfish motives — it is that all men seek to gratify their desires, whatever those desires maybe, with the least exertion. This fundamental law of political economy is, like all other laws of nature, so far as we are concerned, supreme. It is no more affected by the selfishness or unselfishness of our desires than is the law of gravitation. It is simply a fact.

Chapter 11 — Methods of Political Economy

The human reason has two ways of ascertaining truth. The first of these is that of reasoning from particulars to generals in an ascending line, until we come at last to one of those invariable uniformities that we call laws of nature. This method we call the inductive or *a posteriori*. But when we have reached what we feel sure is a law of nature, and as such true in all times and places, then an easier and more powerful method of ascertaining truth is open to us — the method of reasoning in the descending line from generals to particulars. This is the method that we call the deductive, or *a priori* method. For knowing what is the general law, the invariable sequence that we call a law of nature, we have only to discover that a particular comes under it to know what is true in the case of that particular.

In relation of priority the two methods stand in the order in which I have named them — induction being the first or primary method of applying human reason to the investigation of facts, and deduction being the second or derivative. So far as our reason is concerned, induction must give the facts on which we may proceed to deduction. Deduction can safely be based only on what has been supplied to the reason by induction; and where the validity of this first step is called in question, must apply to induction for proof. Both methods are proper to the careful investigation that we speak of as scientific: induction in its preliminary stages, when it is groping for the law of nature; deduction when it has discovered that law, and is thus able to proceed by a shortcut from the general to the particular, without any further need for the more laborious and, so to speak, uphill method of induction, except to verify its conclusions.

There is a further method of investigation, which consists in a combination of these two original methods of reason, and which has been found most effective in the discovery of truth in the physical sciences. When our induction is so pointed to the existence of a natural law that we are able to form a surmise or suspicion of what it may prove to be, we may tentatively assume the existence of such a law, and proceed to see whether particulars will fall into place in deductions made from it. This is the method of tentative deduction, or hypothesis. Where the application of the inductive method was really needed in what is now called by the "new lights" the "classical" political economy was to test the premises from which its deductions were made, and to clear them of what had no better warrant than the disposition to use political economy to justify existing social arrangements. It was not needed to take the place of the deductive method, where that was applicable. For the deductive method, when applied to the further extension of what has already been validly ascertained, constitutes the most powerful means of extending knowledge that the human mind can avail itself of.

In its use of the deductive method after its premises had been settled, the classical political economy was not in error. The error that gave insecurity to its whole structure lay deeper still, in the insufficient inductions on which those premises rested. But, instead of addressing themselves to these flaws in its accepted premises, the various schools of economists generally classed as inductive have denied that there were any general principles that could with certainty be laid down as the basis for deduction. Thus, if such a question be asked them as, does free trade or protection best promote the general prosperity? Or, what is the best system of land tenure? Or, what is the best system of taxation? Or, what are the limits of governmental interference with industry, or trade union regulations? No general answer can be given. It can only be said that one thing may be best in one place and time, and another in another place and time, so that the matter can be determined only by special investigations.

But to me it seems clear that if political economy can be called a science at all, it must as a science, that is to say from the moment the laws of nature on which it depends are discovered, follow the deductive method of examination, using induction only to test the conclusions thus obtained. For the particulars which are included in its problems are too vast and too complex to admit of any hope of bringing them into order and relation by direct induction.

Now the law of nature which forms the postulate of a true science of political economy is not, as has been erroneously assumed, that men are invariably and universally selfish. As a matter of fact, this is not true. Nor can we abstract from man all but selfish qualities in order to make as the object of our thought on economic matters what has been called the "economic man," without getting what is really a monster, not a man.

The law of nature which is really the postulate of a true science of political economy is that men always seek to gratify their desires with the least exertion, whether those desires are selfish or unselfish, good or bad.

That this is a law of nature we have the highest possible warrant, wider in fact that we can have for any of the laws of external nature, such for instance as the law of gravitation. For the laws of external nature can be apprehended only objectively. But that it is a law of nature that men seek to gratify their desires with the least exertion, we may see both subjectively and objectively. Since man himself is included in nature, we may subjectively reach the law of nature that men seek to gratify their desires with the least exertion, by an induction derived from consciousness of our own feelings and an analysis of our own motives of action; while objectively we may also reach the same law by an induction derived from observation of the acts of others.

Proceeding from a law of nature thus doubly assured, the proper method of a political economy which becomes really a science by its correct apprehension of a fundamental law, is the method of deduction from that law, the method of proceeding from the general to the particular.

Thus, in the main, the science of political economy resorts to the deductive method, using induction for its tests. But in its more common investigations its most useful instrument is a form of hypothesis which may be called that of mental or imaginative experiment, by which we may separate, combine or eliminate conditions in our own imaginations, and thus test the working of known principles. This is a most common method of reasoning, familiar to us all, from our very infancy. It is the great working tool of political economy, and in its use we have only to be careful as to the validity of what we assume as principles.

Chapter 12 — Political Economy As Science and Art

There is found among economic writers much dispute not only as to the proper method of political economy, but also as to whether it should be spoken of as a science or as an art. There are some who have styled it a science, and some who speak of it as both science and art. Others again make substantially the same division, into abstract or theoretical or speculative political economy, upon the one side, and concrete, normative or applied political economy, on the other side.

Into this matter, however, it is hardly worthwhile for us to enter at any length, since the reasons for considering a proper political economy as a science rather than an art have been already given. It is only necessary to observe that where systematized knowledge may be distinguished, as it sometimes is, into two branches, science and art, the proper distinction between them is that one relates to what we call laws of nature; the other to the manner in which we may avail ourselves of these natural laws to attain desired ends.

There may be disputes as to whether there is yet a science of political economy, that is to say, whether our knowledge of the natural economic laws is as yet so large and well digested as to merit the title of science. But among those who recognize that the world we live in is in all its spheres governed by law, there can be no dispute as to the possibility of such a science.

When we have worked out the science of political economy — when we shall have discovered and related the natural laws which govern the production and distribution of wealth, we shall then be in a position to see the effect of human laws and customs. But it does not seem to me that such knowledge can be properly spoken of as an art of political economy. There is a science of astronomy, which has its applications in such arts as those of navigation and surveying; but no art of astronomy; and there is a science of chemistry, which has its applications in many arts; but no art of chemistry. And so the science of political economy finds its applications in politics and its various subdivisions. But these applications can hardly be spoken of as constituting an art of political economy.

Yet if we choose, as some have done, to speak of political economy as both science and art, then the art of political economy is the art of securing the greatest production and the fairest distribution of wealth; the art whose proper object is to abolish poverty and the fear of poverty, and so lift the poorest and weakest of mankind above the hard struggle to live. For if there be an art of political economy, it must be the noble art that has for its object the benefit of all members of the economic community.

But just as when men believed in magic they held that there was both white magic and black magic — an art which aimed at alleviating suffering and doing good, and an art which sought knowledge for selfish and evil ends — so, in this view, it may be said that there is a white political economy and a black political economy. Where a knowledge of the laws of the production and distribution of wealth is used to enrich a few at the expense of the many, or even when a reputed knowledge of those laws is used to bolster up such injustice, and by darkening counsel to prevent or delay the reform of it, such art of political economy, real or reputed, is truly a black art. This is the art of which the great Turgot spoke.

For our part, having seen the nature and scope of the science of political economy, for which we adopt the older definition — the science that investigates the nature of wealth and the laws of its production and distribution — let us proceed in this order, endeavoring to discover: 1) the nature of wealth; 2) the laws of its production; and then 3) the laws of its distribution. When this is done we shall have accomplished all that is necessary for a true science of political economy as I understand it.

Part II — The Nature of Wealth

Chapter 1 — Confusions as to the Meaning of Wealth

The purpose of the science of political economy is, as we have seen, the investigation of the laws that govern the production and distribution of wealth in social or civilized life. In beginning its study, our first step is therefore to see what is the nature of the wealth of societies or communities; to determine exactly what we mean by the word wealth when used as a term in political economy.

There are few words in more common use than the word wealth, and in the general way that suffices for ordinary purposes we all know what we mean by it. But when it comes to defining that meaning with the precision necessary for the purposes of political economy, so as to determine what is and what is not properly included in the idea of wealth as political economy must treat of it, most of us, though we often and easily use the word in ordinary thought and speech, are apt to become conscious of indefiniteness and perplexity.

This is not strange. Indeed, it is a natural result of the transference to a wider economy of the term we are accustomed to use in a narrower economy. In our ordinary talk and speech, referring, as it most frequently does, to every-day affairs and the relations of individuals with other individuals, the economy with which we are usually concerned and have most frequently in mind is individual economy, not political economy — the economy whose standpoint is that of the unit, not the economy whose standpoint is that of the social whole or social organism.

The original meaning of the word wealth is that of plenty or abundance; that of the possession of things conducive to a certain kind of weal or well-being. Health, strength and wealth express three kinds of weal or well-being.

In the economy of individuals or social units, everything is regarded as wealth the possession of which tends to give wealthiness, or the command of external things that satisfy desire, to its individual possessor, even though it may involve the taking of such things from other individuals. But in the other economy, that of social wholes, or the social organism, nothing can be regarded as wealth that does not add to the wealthiness of the whole. An individual, for instance, may be wealthy by virtue of obligations due to him from other individuals; but such obligations constitute no part of the wealth of the society, which includes both debtor and creditor. Or, an individual may increase his wealth by robbery or by gaming; but the wealth of the social whole, which comprises robbed as well as robber, loser as well as winner, cannot be thus increased.

It is therefore no wonder that men accustomed to use the word wealth in its ordinary sense, a sense in which no one can avoid its continual use, should be liable, unless they take great care, to slip into confusion when they come to use the same word in its economic sense. But what does seem strange is that indefiniteness, perplexity and confusion as to the meaning of the economic term wealth are even more obvious in the writings of professional economists.

Adam Smith, who is regarded as the founder of the modern science of political economy, is not very definite or entirely consistent as to the real nature of the wealth of nations, or wealth in the economic sense. But since his time the confusion of which he shows traces, instead of being cleared up by the writings of those who in our schools and colleges are recognized as political economists, has become progressively so much worse confounded that in the latest and most elaborate of these treatises all attempts to define the term seem to have been abandoned.

Many of the best-known writers on political economy make no attempt to give any definition of wealth. The same thing is to be said of the two volumes of Karl Marx entitled *Capital;* and also of the two volumes on the same subject by Böhm-Bawerk, which are much quoted by that now dominant school of scholastic political economy known as the "Austrian". And while many other writers, who make no attempt to define wealth, do have a good deal to say about it, what they say is too diffused and incoherent either to quote or condense. There are many who without saying so, evidently hold the opinion thus frankly expressed by Professor Perry in his *Elements of Political Economy* (1866):

> *This word wealth has been the bane of political economy. It is the bog whence most of the mists have arisen which have beclouded the whole subject. From its indefiniteness and the variety of associations it carries along with it in different minds, it is totally unfit for any scientific purpose whatever. It is itself almost impossible to be defined, and consequently can serve no useful purpose in the definition of anything else... The meaning of the word wealth has never been settled; and if political economy must wait until that work be done as a preliminary, the science will never be satisfactorily constructed... Men may think, and talk, and write, and dispute till doomsday, but until they come to use words with definiteness, and mean the same thing by the same word, they reach comparatively few results and make but little progress. And it is just at this point that we find the first grand reason of the slow advance hitherto made by this science. It undertook to use the word for scientific purposes which no amount of manipulation and explanation could make suitable for that service. Happily there is no need to use this word. In emancipating itself from the word wealth as a technical term, political economy has dropped a clog and its movements are now relatively free.*

Now, wealth is the object-noun, or name given to the subject-matter, of political economy, the science that seeks to discover the laws of the production and distribution of wealth in human society. It is therefore the economic term of the first importance. Unless we know what wealth is, how can we possibly hope to discover how it is procured and distributed? Yet after a century of what passes for the cultivation of the science, with professors of political economy in every college, the question, "What is wealth?" finds no certain answer. Even to such questions as, "is wealth material or immaterial?" or "is it something external to man or does it include man and his attributes?" we get no undisputed reply. There is not even a consensus of opinion. And in the latest and most pretentious scholastic teaching the attempt to obtain any has been virtually, where not definitely, abandoned, and the economic meaning of wealth reduced to that of anything having value to the social unit.

It is clear that failure to define its subject-matter or object-noun must be fatal to any attempted science; for it shows lack of the first essential of a true science. And the fate of rejection even by those who profess to study and teach it has already befallen political economy at the hands of the accredited institutions of learning. This fact will not be obvious to the ordinary reader, for it is concealed to him under a change in the meaning of a word.

Chapter 2 — Causes of Confusion as to the Meaning of Wealth

Since the term comes into our language from the Greek, the proper word for expressing the idea of relationship to political economy is "politico-economic." But this is a term too long, and two alien to the the Saxon genius of our mother tongue, for frequent repetition. And so the word "economic" has come into accepted use in English, as expressing that idea. We are justified therefore, in supposing, and as a matter of fact to do generally suppose when we first hear of them, that the works now written by the professors of political economy in our universities and colleges, and entitled "Elements of Economics," or "Principles of Economics," are treatises on political economy. Examination, however, will show that many of these are at least not in reality treatises on the science of political economy, but treatises on what their authors might better call the science of exchanges, or the science of exchangeable quantities. This is not the same thing as political economy, but quite a different thing — a science in short akin to the science of mathematics. In this there is no necessity for distinguishing between what is wealth to the unit and what is wealth to the whole — and moral questions, that must be met in a true political economy, may be easily avoided by those to whom they seem awkward.

A proper name for this totally different science, which the professors of political economy are in so many of the leading colleges and universities on both sides of the Atlantic have now substituted in their teaching for the science they are officially supposed to expound, would be that of "catallactics," as proposed by Archbishop Whately, or that of "plutology," as proposed by Professor Hern, of Melbourne; but it is certainly not properly "economics," for that by long usage is identified with political economy.

The neglect of political economy in the classical world has been explained by modern economists as due to the effect of slavery in causing labor to be regarded as degrading.

But in this a quicker and more direct effect of slavery in preventing the cultivation of political economy has been overlooked. Except perhaps as the crucified fomenter of a servile rebellion, the only class in which any philosopher of the ancient world might have got a hearing that could have brought his name and teachings down to us, was the wealthy class, whose riches were largely in their slaves. For any social condition in which privilege and wealth are inequitably distributed, what Jefferson said of Jesus must be true of all moral or economic teachers — "all the learned of His country, intrenched in its power and riches, were opposed to Him, lest His labors should undermine their advantages."

The first question which a coherent political economy must answer is, "What is wealth?" This, in a state of society in which the ruling class were universally slaveholders, was too delicate a question for any accredited philosopher to have fairly met. Even the most astute among them could do no further than to say, with the intellectual giant Aristotle, that wealth "is all things whose value is measured by money," or with the Roman jurist Ulpian, "that is wealth which can be bought and sold." From this point, the very point to which are modern political economy has in current scholastic teachings now come again, though there may be economies of finance and economies of exchanges, there was and could be no political economy.

But this indisposition to recognize the distinction between what may be wealth to the individual and what is wealth to the society, which has prevented the growth of any science of political economy, has not ceased to show itself with the abolition of chattel slavery — only one of the means by which individuals become wealthy without increase in the general wealth. As it has, in modern civilization, lost importance, other means to the same end have taken its place. But wherever and from what ever causes society is divided into the very rich and very poor, the primary question of political economy, what is wealth? must be a delicate one to men sensibly or insensibly influenced by the feelings and opinions of the dominating class. For in such social conditions much that commonly passes for wealth must really be only legalized robbery, and nothing can be more offensive to those enjoying the profit of robbery than to call it by its true name.

In the preliminary remarks to his *Principles of Political Economy,* John Stuart Mill says:

> *It often happens that the universal belief of one age of mankind – a belief from which no one was, nor without an extraordinary effort of genius and courage, could at that time be free – becomes to a subsequent age so palpable an absurdity, that the only difficulty then is to imagine how such a thing can ever have appeared credible. It has so happened with the doctrine that money is synonymous with wealth. The conceit seems too preposterous to be thought of as a serious opinion. It looks like one of the crude fancies of childhood, instantly corrected by a word from any grown person. But let no one feel confident that he should have escaped the delusion if he had lived at the time when it prevailed.*

Let no one be confident indeed!

Yet it is a mistake to liken the absurdities of the mercantile or protective system to the crude fancies of childhood. This has never been their origin for their strength. In the petty commerce in marbles and tops that goes on among school-boys no boy ever imagined that the more he gave and less he got in such exchange the better off he should be. No primitive people were ever yet so stupid as to suppose that they could increase their wealth by taxing themselves. Any child that could understand the proposition would see that a dollar's worth of gold could not be more valuable than a dollar's worth of anything else. Such ideas are not the fantasies of childhood. Their strength, their persistence, is due to the growth of special interests and artificial restrictions on trading as a means of increasing individual wealth at the expense of the general wealth.

The power of a special interest, though inimical to the general interest, so to influence thought as to make fallacies pass as truths, is a great fact without which neither the political history of our own time and people nor that of other times and peoples can be understood. A comparatively small number of individuals brought into virtual though not necessarily formal agreement of thought and action by something that makes them individually wealthy without adding to the general wealth, may exert an influence out of all proportion to their numbers. A special interest of this kind is, to the general interests of society, as a standing army is to an unorganized mob. It gains intensity and energy in its specialization, and in the wealth it takes from the general stock finds power to mold opinion. Leisure and culture and the circumstances and conditions that command respect accompany wealth, and intellectual ability is attracted by it. On the other hand, those who suffer from the injustice that takes from the many to enrich the few, are in that very thing deprived of the leisure to think, and the opportunities, education and graces necessary to give their thought acceptable expression. They are necessarily the "unlettered," the "ignorant," the "vulgar," prone in their consciousness of weakness to look out for leadership and guidance to those who have the advantages that the possession of wealth can give.

Now, if we consider it, injustice and absurdity are simply different aspects of incongruity. That which to right reason is unjust must be to right reason absurd. But an injustice that impoverishes the many to enrich the few shifts the centers of social power, and thus controls the social organs and agencies of opinion and education. Growing in strength and acceptance by what it feeds on, it has only to continue to exist to become at length so vested or rooted, in that constitution of opinions, beliefs and habits of thought which we take from our social environment, that it is not perceived as injustice or uncertainty, but seems even to the philosopher as an integral part of the natural order.

When an incongruous substance, such as for instance a bullet, is implanted in the human body, the physical system, as soon as it despairs of its removal, sets about the endeavor to accommodate itself to the incongruity, frequently with such success that at length the incongruity is not noticed. The stout, masterful man with whom I have just now been talking, and whom you might liken to a bull were it not for the intelligence of his face, has long carried a bullet under his skin. And men have even been known to live for years with bullets in their brains.

So, too, with philosophical systems. When an incongruity is accepted in a philosophical system, the abilities of its professors are at once set to work to accommodate other parts of the system to the incongruity, frequently with such success that philosophical systems containing fatal incongruities have been known to command acceptance for long generations. Indeed the artificialities and confusions by which an incongruity is made tolerable to a philosophic system, for the very reason that they cannot be understood except by those who have submitted their minds to a special course of cramping, become to them a seeming evidence of superiority, gratifying a vanity like that of the contortionist who has painfully learned to walk a little way on his hands instead of his feet and to twist his body into unnatural and unnecessary positions; or like that of the conveyancer or lawyer, who has in the same way painfully learned to perform such tricks with language.

This, I think, is what was meant in the concise but deep philosophy of Christ by such sayings as that the Kingdom of Heaven, or system of right-doing, though revealed unto babes, is hidden from those deemed wise and prudent, and that what the common people heard gladly was foolishness to the learned Scribes and Pharisees.

But not to depart from the matter in hand: it is evident that the efforts of able men to bring into some semblance of coherency the system of political economy destitute of any clear and coherent definition of wealth must have surrounded the subject with greater perplexities and helped powerfully to prevent the need of a definition of wealth from being felt.

This is precisely what we see when we examine the different attempts to define wealth in the economic sense, and note the increasing confusions that have attended them, culminating in the acceptance of the common meaning of the word wealth — anything that has exchangeable power — as the only meaning that can be given to the economic term; and the consequent abandonment of the possibility of a science of political economy.

Nor can this power of a great pecuniary interest to affect thought, and especially to affect thought in those circles of society whose opinions are most respected, ever be done away with save by the abolition of its cause — the social adjustment or institution that gives power to obtain wealth without earning it. The pecuniary interest in the ownership of slaves was never very large in United States. But it so dominated the thought of the whole country that up to the outbreak of the Civil War the term abolitionist was to good, kindly and intelligent people even in the North an expression that meant everything vile and wicked. And whatever else might have been the issue of the war, had the pecuniary interest in the maintenance of slavery remained, it would still have continued to show itself in thought. But as soon as the supplies of the slave-owning interest were cut off by the freeing of the slaves, this power upon opinions vanished. Now, no preacher, professor or politician, even in the South, would think of advocating or defending slavery; and in Boston, where he narrowly escaped mobbing, stands a public statute of William Lloyd Garrison.

Chapter 3 — Adam Smith and the French Physiocrats

If, considering the increasing indefiniteness among professed economists as to the nature of wealth, we compare Adam Smith's great book with the treatises that have succeeded it, we may observe on its very title-page something usually unnoticed but really very significant. Adam Smith does not propose an inquiry into the nature and causes of wealth, but "an inquiry into the nature and causes of the wealth of nations."

These words have become the descriptive title of the book. Yet the limiting words, "of nations," seem to have been little noticed and less understood by the writers who in increasing numbers for almost a hundred years have taken this great book as a basis for their elucidations and supposed improvements. Their assumption seems to be that it is wealth generally or wealth without limitation which Adam Smith treats of and which is the proper subject of political economy, and that if he meant anything by his determining words "of nations," he referred to such political divisions as England, France, Holland, etc.

Yet it is certain that what he meant by "the wealth of nations," of the nature and causes of which he proposed to inquire, was something essentially different from what is meant by wealth in the ordinary sense of the word, which includes as well everything that may give wealthiness to the individual. It was that kind of wealth the production of which increases and the destruction of which decreases the wealth of society as a whole, which he sought to distinguish from the word "wealth" in its common or individual sense by the limiting words, "of nations," in the meaning not of the larger political divisions of mankind, but of societies or social organisms.

It has been much complained of Adam Smith that he does not define what he means by wealth. But this has been exaggerated.

In the very first paragraph of the introduction to his work he thus explains what he means by the wealth of nations, the only sense of the word wealth which it is the business "of what is properly called political economy" to consider:

> *The annual labor of every nation is the fund which originally supplies it with all the necessities and conveniences of life which it annually consumes, and which consist always either in the immediate produce of that labor, or in what is purchased with that produce from other nations.*

Again, in the last sentence of this introduction he speaks of the "real wealth, the annual produce of the land and labor of the society." And in other places throughout the book he also speaks of this wealth of society or wealth of nations, or real wealth, as the produce of land and labor.

Through the first and most important part of his work, this is the idea which Smith has constantly in mind and to which he constantly adheres in tracing all production of wealth to labor. But having grasped this idea of the nature of wealth without having clearly defined its relation to other ideas is still lying in his mind, he falls into the subsequent confusion of also classing personal qualities and debts as wealth.

Quesnay and the Physiocrats

Francois Quesnay, a French philosopher, was born on June 4, 1694, twenty-eight years before Adam Smith, at Mercy, some ten leagues from Paris. Beginning life in the manual labor of the farm, he was without either the advantages or, as they often prove to men of parts, the disadvantages of a scholastic education. With much effort he taught himself to read, became apprenticed to a surgeon, and at length began practice for himself at Mantes, where he acquired some means and came to the knowledge of Marshal de Noailles, who spoke of him to the Queen, who in her turn recommended him to the King. He finally settled in Paris, bought the place of physician to the King, and was made by the monarch his first physician. Abstaining from the intrigues of the court, he won the sincere respect of Louis XV, with whom as his first physician he was brought into close personal contact. The King made him a noble, gave him a coat of arms, assigned him apartments in the palace, calling him affectionately his thinker, and had his books printed in the royal printing-office. And around him, in his apartments in the palace of Versailles, this "King's Thinker" was accustomed to gather a group of eminent men who joined him in the grandest aim the human mind can entertain — nothing less than the establishment of liberty and the abolition of poverty among man, by the confirmation of human laws to the natural order intended by the Creator.

These men saw what has often been forgotten amid the complexities of a high civilization, but is yet as clear as the sun at noonday to whoever considers first principles. They saw that there is but one source on which men can draw for all their material needs — land; and that there is but one means by which land can be made to yield to their desires — labor. All real wealth, they therefore saw, is the result or product of the application of labor to land.

They had not only grasped this first principle — from which any true economy, even that of the savage tribe or an isolated individual, must start — but they had grasped the central principle of a true political economy. This is the principle that in the natural growth of the social organism into which men are integrated in society there is developed a fund which is the natural provision for the natural needs of that organism — a fund which is not merely sufficient for all the material wants of society, and may be taken for that purpose, its intended destination, without depriving the unit of anything rightfully his; but which must be so taken to prevent the gravest injuries to individuals and the direst disasters to the state.

This fund Quesnay and his followers styled the *produit net* — the net, or surplus, or remaining, product. They called it this, evidently because they saw it as something which remained, attached, as it were, to the control of land, after all the expenses of production that were resolvable into compensation for the exertion of individual labor are paid. What they really meant by the *produit net,* is precisely what is properly understood in English by the word "rent" when used in the special sense which it has acquired since Ricardo's time as a term of political economy.

In grasping the real meaning and intent of the net product, or economic rent, there was opened to the Physiocrats a true system of political economy — a system of harmonious order and beneficent purpose. They had grasped the key without which no true science of political economy is possible, and from the refusal to accept which the scholastic economy that has succeeded Adam Smith is, after nearly a hundred years of cultivation, during which it has sunk into the contemptible position of "the dismal science," now slipping into confessed incompetency and rejection.

But, misled by defective observation and a habit of thought that prevailed long after them, and indeed yet largely prevails, the Physiocrats failed to perceive that economic rent may attach to land used for any purpose. Looking for some explanation in natural law of what was then doubtless generally assumed to be fact, that agriculture is the only occupation which yields to the landlord an unearned increment (rent), they not unnaturally under the circumstances hit upon a striking difference between agriculture, which grows things, and the mechanical and trading occupations, which merely change things in form, place or ownership, as furnishing the explanation for which they sought. This difference lies in the use which agriculture makes of the generative or reproductive principle in nature.

This supposed fact, and what seemed to them the rational explanation of it, the Physiocrats expressed in their terminology by styling agriculture the only productive occupation. All other occupations, however useful, they regarded as sterile or barren. They assumed that such occupations give rise to no net produce or unearned increment, merely returning again to the general fund of wealth, or gross product, the equivalent of what they had taken from it, changing the form, place or ownership of material things already in existence.

This was their great and fatal misapprehension, since it has been effectually used to discredit their whole system.

Still, it was not really a vital mistake. That is to say, it made no change in their practical proposals. The followers of Quesnay insisted that agriculture, in which they admitted fisheries and mines, was the only productive occupation, or in other words the only application of labor that added to the sum of wealth; while manufactures and exchange, though useful, were sterile, merely changing the form or place of wealth without adding to its sum. They, however, proposed no restrictions or disabilities whatever on the occupations they thus stigmatized. On the contrary, they were — which the so-called "English free traders" who have followed Adam Smith never yet have been — free traders in the full sense of the term. In their practical proposition, the single tax, they proposed the only means by which the free trade principle can ever be carried to its logical conclusion — the freedom not merely of trade, but of all other forms and modes of production, with full freedom of access to the natural element which is essential to all production. They were the authors of the motto that is in the English use of the phrase *"Laissez faire!"* "Let things alone," has been so emasculated and perverted, but which on their lips was *"Laissez faire, laissez aller,"*

"Clear the ways and let things alone!" This is said to come from the cry that in medieval tournaments gave the signal for combat. The English motto which I take to come closest to the spirit of the French phrase is, "a fair field and no favor!"

Adam Smith and the Physiocrats

The resemblance of the views expressed in Adam Smith's work to those held by the Physiocrats has been noticed by all critics, and both on the side of their opponents and their advocates there have not been wanting intimations that Smith borrowed from them.

It is a mistake to which the critics who are themselves mere compilers are liable, to think that men must draw from one another to see the same truths or to fall into the same errors. Truth is, in fact, a relation of things, which is to be seen independently because it exists independently. Error is perhaps more likely to indicate transmission from mind to mind; yet even that usually gains its strength and permanence from misapprehensions that in themselves have independent plausibility. Such relations of the stars as that appearance in the North which we call the Dipper or Great Bear, or as that in the South which we call the The Southern Cross, are seen by all who scan the starry heavens, though the names by which men know them are various. And to think that the sun revolves around the earth is an error into which the testimony of their senses must cause all men independently to fall, until a first testimony of the senses is corrected by reason applied to wider observations.

In what is most important, I have come closer to the views of Quesnay and his followers than did Adam Smith, who knew the men personally. But in my case there was certainly no derivation from them. I well recall the day when, checking my horse on a rise that overlooks San Francisco Bay, the commonplace reply of a passing teamster to a commonplace question, crystallized, as by lightning-flash, my brooding thoughts into coherency, and I there and then recognized the natural order — one of those experiences that make those who have had them feel that they can vaguely appreciate what mystics and poets have called the "ecstatic vision." Yet at that time I had never heard of the Physiocrats, or even read a line of Adam Smith.

Afterwards, with a great idea of the natural order in my head, I printed a little book, *Our Land and Land Policy,* in which I urged that all taxes should be laid on the value of land, irrespective of improvements. Casually meeting on a San Francisco street a scholarly lawyer, we stopped to chat and he told me that what I had in my little book proposed was what the French "Economists" a hundred years before had proposed.

I forget many things, but the place where I heard this, and the tones and attitude of the man who told me of it, are photographed on my memory. For, when you have seen a truth that those around you do not see, it is one of the deepest of pleasures to hear of others who have seen it.

What Adam Smith meant by the wealth of nations is in most cases, and wherever he is consistent, the material things produced from land by labor which constitute the necessities and conveniences of human life; the aggregate produce of society, using the word produce as expressive of the sum of material results, in the same way that we speak of agricultural produce, of factory produce, of the produce of mines, or fisheries, or the chase. Now this is what the Physiocrats meant by wealth, or as they sometimes termed it, the gross product of land and labor.

But this is also, as I shall hereafter show, the primary or root meaning of the word wealth in its common use. And whoever will read Smith's "Considerations Concerning the First Formation of Languages," originally published with his "Moral Sentiments," in

1759, will see from his manner of tracing words to their primary uses, that whenever he came to think of it he would have recognized the original and true meaning of the word wealth to be that of the necessities and conveniences of human life, brought into being by the exertion of labor upon land.

The difference between Smith and the Physiocrats is this:

The Physiocrats, on their part, clearly laid down and steadily contended that nothing that did not have material existence, or was not produced from land, could be included in the category of the wealth of society. Adam Smith, however, with seeming inadvertence, has fallen in places into the inconsistency of classing personal qualities and obligations as wealth. This is probably attributable to the fact that what it seemed to him possible to accomplish was much less than the Physiocrats aimed at. The task to which he set himself, that in the main of showing the absurdity and impolicy of the mercantile or protective system, was sufficiently difficult to make him comparatively regardless of speculations that led far beyond it. With the disproval of the current notion that the wealth of nations consists of the precious metals, his care as to what is and what is not a part of that wealth relaxed. He went with the Physiocrats in their condemnation of the attempts of governments to check commerce, but stopped both where they had carried the idea of freeing all production from tax or restraint to the point of a practical proposition, and where they had fallen into obvious error. He neither proposed the single tax, nor did he fall into that mistake of declaring agriculture the only productive occupation. That there is a natural order he saw; and that to this natural order our perceptions of justice conform, he also saw. But that involved in this natural order is a provision for the material needs of advancing society he seems never to have seen.

There are passages in the *Wealth of Nations* where Adam Smith checks his inquiry with a suddenness that shows an indisposition to venture on ground that the possessing classes would deem dangerous. But in nothing he left after him (just before his death he destroyed all manuscripts he did not wish published), is there an indication that he was more than puzzled by the attempt of the Physiocrats to explain the great truth that they saw with wrong apprehension. He clearly perceived that "the produce of labor constitutes the natural recompense or wages of labor," and that it was the appropriation of land that had deprived the laborer of his natural due. But he had evidently never looked further into the phenomena of rent than to see that "the landlords, like all other men, love to reap where they never sowed." He passes over the great subject of the relations of men to the land they inhabit, as though the appropriation by a few of what nature has provided as a dwelling-place and storehouse of all must now be accepted as if it were part of the natural order. And so, indeed, in his times and conditions it must have appeared to him.

That Adam Smith, "all-round man" that he was, possessed both the prudence of the man and the prudence of the philosopher, is shown by the fact that he managed to do what he did, without arousing in greater degree the ire of the defenders of vested wrongs. Whoever will intelligently read the *Wealth of Nations* will find it full of radical sentiment, an arsenal from which lovers of liberty and justice may still draw weapons for victories remaining to be won. Yet its author was a college professor, traveling tutor of a Duke, held a lucrative government position and died Lord Rector of Glasgow University. For the present times at least, the Scotsman succeeded where the Frenchman failed. It is he, not Quesnay, who has come down to us as the "father of political economy."

Chapter 4 — Development of the Scholastic Political Economy

When the first few copies of my *Progress and Poverty* were printed in an author's edition in San Francisco, a large landowner (the late Gen. Beale, proprietor of the Tejon Ranch, and afterwards the United States Minister to Austria), sought me to express the pleasure with which he had read it as an intellectual performance. This, he said, he had felt at liberty to enjoy, for to speak with the freedom of philosophic frankness, he was certain my work would never be heard of by those whom I wished it to affect.

In the same way, but to much greater degree, the small class whom alone the *Wealth of Nations* could first reach were able to enjoy its greatness as an intellectual performance that widened the circle of thought. Few of them were disturbed by any fear of its ultimate effect on special interests. At that time a popular press was not yet in existence, and books of this kind were addressed only to the "superior orders." The House of Commons, the nominal representative of the unprivileged in Great Britain, was filled by the appointees of the great landowners; and the oligarchy that ruled in the British Islands was really stronger than the similar class under the absolute monarchy of France.

Adam Smith had avoided arousing antagonism from the land interests. And in turning the aggressive side of the new science against the protective system, he found favor with, rather than excited prejudice among, the cultured class — the only class to which such a book as his could at that time be addressed. Such a class, under the conditions then existing in Great Britain, is apt to feel a contempt tinged with anger for traders beginning to aspire towards sharing the power and place of "Born masters of the soil."

The larger fact is that Adam Smith, opening the study of political economy at a lower level than the Physiocrats, found less resistance, and his book began to secure so permanent a recognition for the new science that its continuance to our time is properly traced to him as its founder rather than to them.

In 1798, eight years after the author of the *Wealth of Nations,* lamenting with his last breath that he had done so little, was laid to rest in the Edinburgh Cannongate, the English clergyman Malthus brought forward his famous theory of population. This at once, like "a long-felt want," took its place in the crystallizing system of political economy which Smith had brought into shape, and which, if it was lacking in a clear and consistent definition of wealth, was not on that account objectionable to the spirit of the learned institutions. A few years after Malthus came Ricardo, to correct mistakes into which Smith had fallen as to the nature and cause of rent, and to formulate the true law of rent; but to do this by laying stress on the fact that rent would increase as the necessities of increasing population forced cultivation to less and less productive land, or to lessen less productive points on the same land.

When Adam Smith, as though fearful of the radical conclusions to which it must lead, abandoned his true perception that "the produce of labor constitutes the natural recompense or wages of labor," he fell into a theory of wages which considered the master as providing from his capital the wages of his workman. This, together with the theory of the tendency of population to increase faster than subsistence, and the apprehension of the theory of rent as resulting from the forcing of exertion to less and less productive land, became cardinal doctrine. These, linking with and buttressing each other, in what soon became the accepted system of political economy as developed from the *Wealth of Nations,* did away effectually with any fear that the study of natural laws of the production and distribution of wealth might be dangerous to the great House of Have.

In textbooks and teachings from which Adam Smith's recurring perceptions of the natural equality of men were eliminated, it became indeed "the dismal science." It was held by its admirers that it needed only to be sufficiently taught them to convince even the "lower orders," that things as they are are things as they ought to be, except perhaps that "the monopolizing spirit of merchants and manufacturers," and "the sneaking arts of underling tradesmen" should no longer be permitted to be erected into maxims for governmental interferences with trade.

Thus as the system of political economy presented by Adam Smith began to attract the attention of the thoughtful and cultured, it did not meet the resistance it would have encountered had the special interests which it threatened really been those of the growing class of merchants and manufacturers. On the other hand, the apparent turning of its aggressive side against merchants and manufacturers prevented the powerful landed interest from perceiving fully its relation to their own monopoly until it had gained the weight of recognized philosophic authority.

The repeal of the English corn-laws passed in Great Britain for a victory of free trade as far as it was practicable to carry free trade. And in scholastic circles in that country and in the United States, and throughout the civilized world that took its intellectual impulse from England, it greatly increased the hopefulness of the professed economists.

Thus strengthened by this powerful impulse, there continued to grow up under the sanction and development of a series of able and authoritatively placed men, whose efforts were devoted to smoothing away difficulties and covering up incongruities, an accredited system of political economy which found its most widely accepted expounder in John Stuart Mill, and reached perhaps its highest point of authority in scholastic circles about or shortly after the centennial of the publication of the *Wealth of Nations.* Yet it was as wanting in coherence as the image that Nebuchadnezzar saw in his dream. It contained much real truth well worked out. But this was conjoined with fallacies which could not stand examination. The attempt to define its object-noun, wealth, and the sub-term of wealth, capital, made them much more indefinite and confused than they had been left by Adam Smith. And it was never attempted to bring together what were given as the laws of the distribution of wealth — as that would have shown at a glance their want of relation. This political economy had no real hold on common thought, and was regarded even by ordinarily intelligent men as a scholastic or esoteric science. But it was spoken of by its professors with the utmost confidence as an assured science, and their belief in its success was greatly increased.

From the beginning until well past the middle of the nineteenth century the temper of the recognized expounders of the political economy which took shape from Adam Smith's foundation was hopeful and confident. They believed they had hold of a true science, which needed only development to be universally recognized. Thus Colonel Torrens, in the introduction to his *Essay on the Production of Wealth,* says in 1821:

> *In the progress of the human mind, a period of controversy among the cultivators of any branch of science must necessarily precede the period of unanimity. With respect to political economy, the period of controversy is passing away, and that of unanimity rapidly approaching. Twenty years hence there will scarcely exist a doubt respecting any of its fundamental principles.*

With the great defeat of protection in 1846, the confidence of political economists became even greater than before. But the predictions that the example of Great Britain in abolishing protective duties would be quickly followed throughout the civilized world were not realized; and fostered by such tremendous political events as the great fight between the American States and the Franco-German war, the wave of reaction in favor of protection seemed to sweep over pretty nearly all the civilized world.

And while in the scholastic world, of the English-speaking countries at least, the triumph of Adam Smith's opposition to the principles of the mercantile system seemed to have established firmly an accepted science of political economy, and chairs for its teaching formed an indispensable adjunct of every institution of education, the real incoherencies which had been slurred over began more and more to show themselves.

The reason for the constantly increasing confusion of the scholastic political economy has lain in the failure of the so-called science to define its subject-matter or object-noun. Statistics cannot aid us in the search for things until we know what it is we want to find. It is the Tower of Babel over again. Men who attempt to develop a science of the production and distribution of wealth without first deciding what they mean by wealth cannot understand each other or even understand themselves.

Chapter 5 — Gropings Toward a Determination of Wealth

Yet such was the feeling that there ought to be a political economy, and so agreeable to the ruling class was what was offered as such, that chairs for the study of it began to multiply. And as nearly every professor of political economy thought it incumbent on him to write a textbook, or at least to do something to show a reason for his existence, there was much going over old ground and picking out small differences, but no questioning of anything that could arouse vital debate. And given a state of society in which the many were poor and the few were rich, any attempt to point out the true political economy, if it got attention, would inevitably arouse much debate.

Thus in fact political economy, as it found teachers and professors and the standing of a science, was a very comfortable doctrine to the class who had appropriated land as belonging to them exclusively. It applied the doctrine of "letting things alone," without any suggestion of the question of how things came to be. It was, as it was styled by Clement C. Biddle, the American translator of Say, "the liberal doctrine that the most active, general and profitable employments are given to the industry and commerce of every people by allowing to their direction and application the most perfect freedom compatible with the security of property." As to what constitutes property there was no dispute. And if one did not look too closely, and beyond the usages of the times, in the more advanced European nations there could be no dispute. Property? Why property was of course what was susceptible of ownership. Any fool would know that!

The question of the validity of property was never really raised in England until after the publication of *Progress and Poverty* began to call it up. But the attention which that has aroused has since brought to light some definite utterances, which show, as I take it, that the doctrines of the French Physiocrats would have found hospitable reception in Great Britain had it been possible at the time to have really made them known.

Thus H. M. Hyndman has dug up from the British Museum a lecture by Thomas Spence, delivered before the Philosophical Society of Newcastle, a year prior to the publication of the *Wealth of Nations*, and for which to the Society, as Spence puts it, did him "the honor" to expel him. In this lecture Spence declares that all men "have as equal and just a property in land as they have in liberty, air, or the light and heat of the sun," and he proposes that the value of land should be taken for all public expenses, and all other taxes of whatever kind and nature should be abolished. He draws a glowing picture of what humanity would be if this simple but most radical reform were adopted. But so much was he against the wishes of all that had authority, his proposal was utterly forgotten until dug out of its burial-place more than a century after.

So, in 1889, D. C. MacDonald, a single-tax man, and the solicitor of Aberdeen, dug out of the Advocates' Library of Edinburgh, and the British Museum, in London, copies of a book printed in 1782 by William Ogilvie, Professor of Humanities in Kings College, Aberdeen, entitled *An Essay on the Right of Property in Land, with Respect to its Foundation in the Law of Nature, its Present Establishment by the Municipal Laws of Europe, and the Capital Regulations by which it Might be Rendered More Beneficial to the Lower Ranks of Mankind.* Professor Ogilvie, though he makes no reference to any other authority than that of Moses, had evidently some knowledge of the Physiocrats, and most unquestionably declares that land is *a birthright which every citizen still retains.* He advocates the taxation of land, with the entire abolition of all other taxes, though, as if despairing of so radical a reform, he proposes some palliatives such as allotments to actual settlers, leases, etc.

He doubtless saw the utter hopelessness of making the fight under existing conditions, for it seems probable that his book was never published, only a few copies being printed for private circulation by the author.

Among the scholastically accepted writers in the first thirty years of the century are two who seem to have some glimmerings of the truth perceived by the Physiocrats, of the relations between land and labor, though in a curiously distorted way. Dr. Chalmers, who was a divinity professor in the University of Edinburgh, and a strong Malthusian, contended that the owners of land ultimately paid all taxes levied on labor, and contended that Titles (which he regarded as so much retained by the state for beneficial purposes) should be maintained. All others he would have ultimately abolished, and the revenues of the state ultimately raised from the value of land. This, he thought, would be simpler and better, and avoid much dispute, "relieving government from the odium of taxes which so endanger the cause of order and authority." He was a staunch supporter of primogeniture, opposed to anything which aimed at the division of the land, and would have the country enjoy the spectacle of the noble and splendid aristocracy. And while he would have the landlords pay all taxes, he thought it "wholesome and befitting that they should have the political ascendancy also." For "the lords of the soil, we repeat, are naturally and properly the lords of the ascendant."

Another curious example of the perversion of the doctrine of the relation between land and labor was given by Edward Gibbon Wakefield, who visited this country in its more democratic days in the first quarter of the century. He was impressed with the differences between the society growing up here and that to which he had been used, and viewing everything from the standpoint of those accustomed to look on the rest of mankind as created for their benefit, he deemed the great social and economic disadvantage of the United States to be "the scarcity of labor." How could an English gentlemen emigrate to a country where he might actually have to black his own boots, and where no one could count on a constant supply of labor, ready to accept as a boon any opportunity to perform the most menial and degrading service? He saw, as Adam Smith before him saw, that this "scarcity of labor" came from the cheapness of land where the vast area of the public domain was open for settlement at nominal prices. Without the slightest question that the land was made for landlords, and that laborers were intended to furnish a supply of labor for the upper classes, he wished to bring about in these new countries such salutary "scarcity of employment" as would give cheap and abundant labor from the very start of settlement. He, therefore, proposed that land should not be given, but sold at the outset, at what he called a sufficient price — a price high enough to make laborers work for others until they acquired the fund necessary to pay a price for what nature offered without money and without price. The money received by the state in this way he proposed to devote in paying the passage of suitable and selected immigrants.

This plan was very attractive to the more wealthy and influential class of Englishmen concerned in, or thinking of, emigrating to the newer colonies, and was finally adopted by the corporation concerned in settling West Australia, and afterwards the other Australian colonies. But even its obvious inferences never affected the teaching of political economy.

In 1850 two works appeared in England which were both premonitions of upcoming demand for a political economy which would take some consideration of the interests of the masses. One of these was by Herbert Spencer, then young and unknown, and was entitled *Social Statics, or the Conditions Essen-*

5. Gropings Toward a Determination of Wealth tial to Human Happiness Specified, and the First of Them Developed. Chapter IX of this book, "the right to the use of the earth," is a telling denial of what the economists of Smith's school had quietly assumed could not be questioned, the validity of property in land. It got no attention in England. It was however reprinted in the United States in 1864, with a note by the author, and when, about 1877, Appleton & Co., of New York, became the American publishers of his philosophical writings, they reprinted this with his other works and on the strength of them it began to get into circulation.

This was the only work of the kind I knew when writing *Progress and Poverty*. In *A Perplexed Philosopher* (1892), I have given a full account of it, and of Mr. Spencer's shifting repudiation and final recantation of what he had said in denial of property in land.

Some notion of the incongruity of the idea that a small fraction of mankind were intended to eat, and eat luxuriously without working, and another and far larger portion to have nothing but work to enable them to eat, and be compelled to beg as a boon the opportunity to do that, runs in broken flashes through much of the reform literature. But in political economy as it up to 1880 existed all such questioning was tabooed, and the utmost that could be found in any of the writers recognized by the schools was a timid suggestion that the future unearned increment of land values might sometime be recognized as belonging to the community, a proposition that, though it amounted to nothing whatever, as landlords were ready to sell land for what would give them any unearned increment not yet in sight, caused John Stuart Mill, who had been giving some adhesion to it, to be looked on askance by some, as an awful radical.

The struggle for the repeal of the corn laws in England did not lead to any development of a protectionist political economy. Books and pamphlets enough were written in favor of protection, but they were merely appeals to old habits of thought and vulgar prejudices, and the forces in favor of repeal carried them down.

Elsewhere, however, it was different. On the Continent the conditions under which the tentative victory of free trade was won in England were lacking. Cut up into hostile nations, burdened with demands for revenue, the mercantile system got a practical hold that could not be broken by the halfhearted measures of its English opponents, and the claim of hope which came with the English-French treaty negotiated between Cobden and Napoleon III was destroyed by the tremendous struggles which followed the fall of the latter. In Germany the outburst of national feeling which followed the struggles with France and the unification of German states gave rise to a school of German economists who taught a national economy, in which under various names, such as romantic, inductive and national, protectionism was advocated.

When it came to making peace between England and the United States after the War of Independence, the American Commissioners were instructed to stipulate for a complete free trade between the two countries. They failed in this, owing to the prevalence of the protective sentiment in Great Britain at the time. When the Articles of Confederation gave way to the Constitution, the need for an independent source of revenue took the easy means of laying a federal tariff upon foreign productions, though free trade between the States was guaranteed; and the growth of selfish interests caused by and promotive of a constantly increasing demand for greater revenue built up a strong party in favor of protection, which had its way when the slavery question, taking sectional shape, put the States in which protectionism was dominant in control of the government with the secession of the South. This interest sought warrant in a scheme of political economy, and found it in drawing from the German economists and the writings of Henry C. Carey of Philadelphia. In America this protectionist semblance of a political economy had its chief seat in the University of Pennsylvania, and the support of a powerful party in which the ideas of Jefferson were opposed by those of Hamilton.

Among the schools, moreover, there was a divergence which began to assume greater proportions as a success of the anti-corn laws struggle began to be shown in the accomplishment of all that any of its advocates dared to propose. This took shape in a contention as to value, which inclined to emphasize the fact that the admission that somewhat immaterial things were conceded to be wealth, destroyed the ability to keep any immaterial things having value out of that category, and consequently that wealth in the common sense was the only thing to be considered in political economy, which was really a science of exchanges. With the efforts of Jevons, Macleod and others, this began to make way, and was naturally affiliated with the historical, the inductive, the socialistic and other protectionist schools which grew from the Continental teachings. Instead of working for greater directness and simplicity, it really made of political economy an occult science, in which nothing was fixed, and the professors of which, claiming superior knowledge, could support whatever they chose to.

During the century another form of protectionism had been growing up, originating in England, but gaining adherence everywhere. Like the others, it recognized no difference between land and the products of labor, counting them all as wealth, and aimed at the improvement in the conditions of labor. Recognizing the workers as a class naturally separate from employers, it aimed to unite the laborers in combinations, and to invoke in their behalf the power of the state to impose restrictions, shortened hours, and in various ways to serve their interests at the expense of the primarily employing class. This took the form of what passed for a system in Karl Marx's ponderous two volumes entitled *Capital,* written in England in 1867, but published in German and not translated into English until after his death in 1887. Without distinguishing between natural opportunities and products of labor, Marx holds that there are two kinds of value — use value and exchange value — and that through some alchemy of buying and selling, the capitalist who hires men to turn material into products gets a larger value then he gives. Upon this economic proposition of Marx, political schemes with slight variations have been promulgated after the matter of political platforms.

Under the name of socialism, a name which all such movements have now succeeded in appropriating, all such plans are embraced. We sometimes hear of "scientific socialism," as something to be established, as it were, by proclamation, or by act of government. In this there is a tendency to confuse the idea of science with something purely conventional or political, a scheme or proposal, not a science. For science, as previously explained, is concerned with natural laws, not with the proposals of man — with relations which always have existed and always must exist. Socialism takes no account of natural laws, neither seeking them nor striving to be governed by them. It is an art or conventional scheme like any other scheme in politics or government, while political economy is an exposition of certain invariable laws of human nature. The proposal which socialism makes is that the collectivity or state shall assume the management of all means of production, including land, capital and man himself; do away with all competition, and convert mankind into two classes, the directors, taking their orders from government and acting by governmental authority, and the workers, for whom everything shall be provided, including the directors themselves. Modern socialism is more destitute of any central and guiding principle than any philosophy I know of. It has no system of individual rights whereby it can define the extent to which the individual is entitled to liberty or to which the state may go in restraining it. And so long as no individual has any principle of guidance it is impossible that society itself should have any. How such a combination could be called a science, and how it should get a following, can be accounted for only by the "fabled facility of writing without thinking," which the learned German ability of studying details without any leading principle permits to pass, and by the number of places which such a bureaucratic organization would provide. However, through government repression and its falling in with trade-union notions, it has made great headway in Germany, and has taken considerable hold in England.

Chapter 6 — The Breakdown of Scholastic Political Economy

In January, 1880, preceded in 1879 by an author's edition in San Francisco, appeared my *Progress and Poverty,* and it was later followed in the same year by an English edition and a German edition, and in 1882 by cheap paper editions both in England and the United States.

Progress and Poverty has been the most successful economic work ever published. Its reasoning has never been successfully assailed, and on three continents it is given birth to movements whose practical success is only a question of time. Yet though the scholastic political economy has been broken, it has not been, as I at the time anticipated, by some of its professors taking up what I had pointed out; but by a new and utterly incoherent political economy which has taken its place in the schools.

Among the adherents of the scholastic political economy, who had been claiming it as a science, there had been from the time of Smith no attempt to determine what wealth was; no attempt to say what constituted property, and no attempt to make the laws of production or distribution correlate and agree, until there thus burst on them from a fresh man, without either the education or the sanction of the schools, on the remotest verge of civilization, a reconstruction of the science, that began to make its way and command attention. What were their training and laborious study worth if it could be thus ignored, and if one who had never seen the inside of a college should be admitted to prove the inconsistency of what they had been teaching as a science? It was not to be thought of. And so while a few of these professional economists, driven to say something about *Progress and Poverty*, resorted to misrepresentation, the majority preferred to rely upon their official positions in which they were secured by the interests of the dominant class, and to treat as beneath contempt a book circulating by thousands in the three great English-speaking countries and translated into all the important modern languages. Thus the professors of political economy seemingly rejected the simple teachings of *Progress and Poverty*, refrained from meeting with disproof or argument what it had laid down, and treated it with contemptuous silence.

Thus the professors of political economy, having the sanction and support of the schools, preferred to unite their differences, by giving up what had been insisted on as essential, and to teach an incomprehensible jargon, an occult science, which required a great study of what had been written by numerous learned professors all over the world, and a knowledge of foreign languages. So the scholastic political economy, as it had been taught, utterly broke down, and, as taught in the schools, tended to protectionism and the Germans, and to the assumption that it was the recondite science on which no one not having the endorsement of the colleges was competent to speak.

The new science speaks of the "science of economics" and not of "political economy." It teaches that there are no eternally valid natural laws; and, asked if free trade or protection be beneficial or if the trusts be good or bad, declines to give a categorical answer, but replies that this can be decided only as to the particular time and place, and by a historical investigation of all that has been written about it. As such inquiry must, of course, be left to professors and learned men, it leaves the professors of "economics," who have almost universally taken the places founded for professors of "political economy," to dictate as they please, without any semblance of embarrassing axioms or rules.

Such inquiry as I have been able to make of the recently

published works and writings of the authoritative professors of the science has convinced me that this change has been general, in all the colleges, both of England and the United States. So general is this scholastic utterance that it may now be said that the science of political economy, as founded by Adam Smith and taught authoritatively in 1880, has now been utterly abandoned, its teachings being referred to as the teachings of "the classical school" of political economy, now obsolete.

What has succeeded is usually denominated the Austrian school, for no other reason that I can discover than that "far kine have long horns." If it has any principles, I have been utterly unable to find them. The inquirer is usually referred to the incomprehensible works of Professor Alfred Marshall of Cambridge in England, whose first 764-page volume of his *Principles of Economics,* out in 1891, has not yet given place to a second, and to the ponderous works of Eugen V. Böhm-Bawerk, Professor of Political Economy, first at Innsbruck and then at Vienna.

This pseudo-science is admirably calculated to serve the purpose of those powerful interests dominant in the colleges under our organization, that must fear a simple and understandable political economy, and who vaguely wish to have the poor boys who are subjected to it by their professors rendered incapable of thought on economic subjects. There is nothing that suggests so much what Schopenhauer (*Parerga and Paralipomena*) said of the works of the German philosopher Hegel than what the professors have written, and the volumes for mutual admiration which they publish as serials:

> *If one should wish to make a bright young man so stupid as to become incapable of all real thinking, the best way would be to command to him a diligent study of these works. For these monstrous piecings together of words which really destroy and*

contradict one another so causes the mind to vainly torment itself in the effort to discover their meaning that at last it collapses exhausted, with its capacity for thinking so completely destroyed that from that time on meaningless phrases count with it for thoughts.

It is to this state that political economy in the teachings of the schools, which profess to know all about it, has now come.

Chapter 7 — Wealth and Value

We have seen the utter confusion that exists among economists as to the nature of wealth, and have sufficiently shown its causes and results. Let us return now to the question we have in hand, and that must first be settled before we can advance on solid ground: what is the meaning of wealth as an economic term?

The only proposition as to wealth on which we may say that all economists agree is that wealth has value. But as to whether all that has value is wealth, or as to what forms of value are wealth and what are not, there is wide divergence. And if we consider the definitions that are given in accepted works either of the term wealth or of the sub-term of wealth, capital, it will be seen that the confusions as to the nature of wealth which they show seem to proceed from confusions as to the nature of value.

The term value is of most fundamental importance in political economy; so much so that by some writers political economy has been styled at the science of values. Yet in the consideration of the meaning and nature of value we come at once into the very quicksand and fogland of economic discussion — a point which from the time of Adam Smith has been wrapped in increasing confusions and beset with endless controversy. Let us move carefully, for here is a point from which apparently slight divergences may ultimately distort conclusions as to matters of the utmost practical moment.

The original and widest meaning of the word "value" is that of worth or worthiness, which involves and expresses the idea of esteem or regard.

But we esteem some things for their own qualities or for uses to which they may be directly put, while we esteem other things for what they will bring in exchange. We do not distinguish the kind or reason of regard in our use of the word esteem, nor yet is there any need of doing so in our common use of the word value. The sense in which the word value is used is for common purposes sufficiently indicated by the conditions or nature of the thing to which value is attributed. Thus, the one word value has in common English speech two distinct senses. One is that of usefulness or utility — as when we speak of the value of the ocean to man, the value of the compass in navigation or the value of the stethoscope in the diagnosis of disease.

The other and, though derived, utterly distinct sense of the word value, is that of what is described as exchangeability or purchasing power — as when we speak of the value of gold as greater than that of iron; of a book in rigid binding as being more valuable than the same book in plain binding; of the value of a copyright or a patent; or of the lessening in the value of steel by the Bessemer process.

The first sense of the word value, which is that of usefulness, the quality that a thing may have of ministering directly to human needs, was distinguished by Adam Smith as "value in use."

The second sense of the word value, which is that of worth in transfer or trade, the quality that a thing may have of ministering indirectly to human desire through its exchangeability for other things, was distinguished by Adam Smith as "value in exchange."

These two terms, adopted by Adam Smith, as best expressing the two distinct senses of the word value, at once took their place in the accepted economic terminology. But though the terms of distinction which he used have been from the first accepted, this has not been the case with the distinction itself. From the first, his successors and commentators began to question its validity, declaring that nothing could have exchange value for which there was not demand; that demand implied some kind of utility or usefulness, and hence that what has value in exchange must also have value in use; and that Smith had been led into confusion by a disposition to import moral distinctions into a science that knows nothing of moral distinctions.

The capacity of satisfying some desire, no matter how idle, vicious or cruel, is indeed all that is necessary to exchangeability or value in exchange. But to give usefulness or value in use something more is necessary, and that is the capacity to satisfy, not any possible desire, but those desires at which we call needs or wants, and which, lying lower in the order of desires, are felt by all men.

Value in use and value in exchange may and often do attach to the same things. As a matter of fact, doubtless the great majority of things having value in exchange have also value in use. But this connection is not necessary, and the two qualities have no relation whatever to each other. A thing may have use value in the highest degree, yet very little exchange value or none at all. A thing may have exchange value in very high degree and little or no use value. Air has the highest value in use, as without air we could not live a minute. But this supreme utility does not give air exchange value. The Bambino of Rome or the Holy Coat of Treves could probably be exchanged, as similar venerated objects have been at times exchanged, for enormous sums; but the use value of the one is that of a waxen doll baby, that of the other an old rag. The two qualities of value in use and value in exchange are as essentially different and unreliable as are weight and color, though as we sometimes speak of heavy browns and light blues, so do we in common speech use the word value now to express one of these qualities and now the other. The quality of value in use is an intrinsic or inherent quality attaching to the thing itself, and giving it fitness to satisfy man's needs. It cannot have value in use except it has that, and as it has that, no matter what be its value in exchange. And its use value is the same whether much can be obtained for it in exchange or "no one would pick it up." The quality of value in exchange, on the other hand, is not intrinsic or inherent.

There is, to be sure, a special sense in which, conformably to usage, we may speak in certain cases of an intrinsic value. The cases in which we do this are cases in which we wish to distinguish between the exchange value which a thing may have in a higher and more valuable form and the exchange value which still remains if it were reduced to a lower or less valuable form. Thus, a silver pitcher or a United States silver coin would lose exchange value if beaten into ingots. Yet they would retain the exchange value of the metal from which they were made. This value in exchange which would remain in a lower form we are accustomed to speak of as "intrinsic value." But in using this term we should always remember its merely relative sense. Value in the economic sense, or value in exchange, can never really be intrinsic. It refers not to any property of the thing itself, but to an estimate that is placed on it by man — to the toil and trouble that man will undergo to acquire possession of it, or the amount of other things costing toil and trouble that they will give for it.

Nor is there any common measure in the human mind between usefulness and exchangeability. Whether we most esteem a thing for the intrinsic qualities that give it usefulness, or for its intrinsic quality of commanding other things in exchange, depends upon conditions.

A daring fellow recently crossed from the coast of Norway to the United States in a sixteen-foot boat. Supposing him to come to New York, and one of our hundredfold millionaires, in the fashion of an Arabian Nights' Sultan, to say to him: "if you will make a trip at my direction you may fill up your boat at my expense with anything you choose to take from New York regardless of its cost." What would he fill it up with? That could not be answered in a word, as it would entirely depend upon where the millionaire wanted him to go. If he were merely to cross the Hudson River from New York to Jersey City, he would disregard value in use and fill up with what had the highest value in exchange, in comparison to bulk and weight — gold, diamonds, paper money. To carry the more of these he would leave out everything having value in use that he could get along without for an hour or two — even to extra sails, anchor, sea-drag, compass, a morsel of food or drink of water. But if he were to cross the Atlantic again, his first care would be for things useful in the management of his boat and the maintenance of his own life and comfort during the long months of danger and solitude before he could hope again to reach land. He would regard value in use, disregarding value in exchange. If he had not lost the prudence which, no less than daring, is required successfully to make such a trip, it may well be doubted whether he would not prefer to carry its weight in freshwater than to take a single diamond or gold piece and prefer another can of biscuit or condensed beef to the last bundle of thousand-dollar notes that he might take instead.

Adam Smith was right. The distinction between value in use and value in exchange is an essential one. Despite all attempts to confuse and obliterate them, "value in use" and "value in exchange" must still hold their place in economic terminology. The terms themselves are perhaps not the happiest that might be chosen. But so long have they now been used that it would be difficult to substitute anything in their place. It is only necessary to do what Adam Smith could hardly have deemed necessary — point out what they really mean. They were taken indeed by him from common speech, and still retain the great advantage to any economic term of being generally intelligible.

In common speech the one word value, as I have already said, usually suffices to express either value in use or value in exchange. For which sense of the word is meant is ordinarily indicated with sufficient clearness by the context. In cases where the indication is not sufficiently clear, the use of the word "value" will at once provoke a question equivalent to "do you mean value for use or value for exchange?"

In economic reasoning, however, the danger of using one word to represent two distinct and often contrasted ideas is very much greater than in common speech, and if the word is to be retained, one of its senses must be abandoned. Of the two meanings of the word value, the first, that of value in use, is not called for, or called for only incidentally in political economy; while the second, that of value in exchange, is called for continually, for this is the value with which political economy deals. To economize the use of words, while at the same time avoiding the liability to misunderstanding and confusion, it is expedient therefore to restrict the use of the word value, as an economic term, to the meaning of value in exchange, as was done by Adam Smith, and has since his time generally been followed; and to discard the use of the single word value in the sense of value in use, substituting for it where there is occasion to express the idea of value in use, and the close context does not clearly show the limitation of meaning, either the term "value in use" or some such word as usefulness or utility. This I shall endeavor to do in this work — using hereafter the single term value, as meaning purchasing power or "value in exchange."

Chapter 8 — Economic Value: Its Real Meaning and Final Measure

Value, as an economic term, means, as we have seen, value in exchange, or exchangeability. But from what does this quality of value in exchange proceed? And by what may we measure it? Qualities such as size, distance, direction, color and the like are only comprehensible and intelligible to us by reference to some fixed starting point. Size and distance, for instance, are comprehended and intelligibly expressed as relations to certain measures of extension, such as the foot, the meter, diameters of the earth, or diameters of the earth's orbit; or color, as a relation to the order in which certain impressions are received through the human eye; and so on.

Now, has not also the idea of value some fixed starting-point, by which it becomes comprehensible and intelligible, as have all other ideas of relation? Clearly it has. What the idea of value really springs from is the relation of each thing having value to something which is the source and natural measure of all value — namely, human exertion, with its attendant irksomeness or weariness.

Adam Smith saw this, though he may not have consistently held to it, as was the case with some other things he clearly saw for a moment, as through a rift in clouds which afterwards closed up again. In the *Wealth of Nations*, he says:

> *Every man is rich or poor according to the degree in which he can afford to enjoy the necessaries, conveniences and amusements of human life. But after the division of labor has once thoroughly taken place, it is but a very small part of these with which a man's own labor can supply him. The far greater part of them he must derive from the labor of other people, and he must be rich or poor according to the quantity of that labor which he can command,*

or which he can afford to purchase. The value of any commodity, therefore, to the person who possesses it, and who means not to use or consume it himself, but to exchange it for other commodities, is equal to the quantity of labor which it enables him to purchase or command. Labor, therefore, is the real measure of the exchangeable value of all commodities. (Book I, Chapter V)

He repeats this statement a little further on:

Equal quantities of labor, at all times and places, may be said to be of equal value to the laborer. In his ordinary state of health, strength and spirits; in the ordinary degree of his skill and dexterity, he must always lay down the same portion of his ease, his liberty, and his happiness. The price which he pays must always be the same, whatever may be the quantity of goods which he receives in return for it. Of these indeed it may sometimes purchase a greater and sometimes a smaller quantity; but it is their value which varies, not that of the labor which purchases them. At all times and places that is dear which it is difficult to come at, or which it costs much labor to acquire; and that cheap which is to be had easily, or with very little labor. Labor, therefore, never varying in its own value, is alone the ultimate and real standard by which the value of all commodities can at all times and places be estimated and compared. It is their real price; money is their nominal price only.... Labor, therefore, it appears evidently, is the only universal, as well as the only accurate measure of value, or the only standard by which we can compare the values of different commodities at all times and at all places.

How then is it that Adam Smith, when he needed a term which should express the second sense of the word value, did not adopt a phrase that would bring out the fundamental meaning of value in this sense, such, for instance, as "value in toil," or "value in exertion," or "value in labor;" but instead of any of them chose a phrase, "value in exchange," which refers directly to only a secondary and derivative meaning? The reasons he himself gives, in what immediately follows the first two paragraphs I have quoted:

> *But though labor be the real measure of the exchangeable value of all commodities, it is not that by which their value is commonly estimated. It is often difficult to ascertain the proportion between two different quantities of labor. The time spent in two different sorts of work will not always alone determine this proportion. The different degrees of hardship endured, and of ingenuity exercised, must likewise be taken into account. There may be more labor in an hour's hard work than in two hours' easy business; or in an hour's application to a trade which cost ten years' labor to learn, than in a month's industry at an ordinary and obvious employment. But it is not easy to find any accurate measure either of hardship or ingenuity. In exchanging, indeed, the different productions of different sorts of labor for one another, some allowance is commonly made for both. It is adjusted, however, not by any accurate measure, but by the higgling and bargaining of the market, according to that sort of rough equality which, though not exact, is yet sufficient for carrying on the business of common life.*

There are here two reasons assigned for the choice of the term "value in exchange," to denote what Smith saw with perfect, though only momentary clearness, really to mean "value in exertion." The first, and it is a weighty one, is that the term "value in exchange" was already familiar, and would be best understood in bringing out the distinction he wished to dwell upon — the difference between value in the economic sense and "value in use."

The second, which indicates a confusion in the philosopher's own mind — the swiftness with which the clouds drifted over the star he had just seen — is that he could think of nothing by which to measure the toil and trouble of exertion except time of application, which he truly saw could only measure quantity and not quality — that is to say, duration, not intensity. He failed to recognize the obvious fact that if the toil and trouble of exertion dispensed with be the measure of value, then, correlatively, value must be the real measure of the toil and trouble of that exertion, and that the something he was seemingly looking for — some material thing or attribute which, as a yardstick measures length, should measure the toil and trouble of exertion — is not to be found, because it cannot exist, the only possibility of such a measurement lying in "the higgling of the market." For since toil and trouble, which constitute the resistance to exertion, are subjective feelings which cannot be objectively recognized until brought, through their influence upon action, into the objective field, there is no way of measuring them except by the inducement that will tempt men to undergo them in exertion, which can be determined only by competition or "the higgling of the market."

Adam Smith was never called upon to revise or in any way to reconsider the statement of his great book as to the nature of value, the discussion on the subject having arisen since his death. His successors in political economy have been, with few exceptions, not men of original thought, but the mere imitators, compilers and straw-splitters who usually follow a great work of genius. They have, without looking further, accepted the term used by him, "value in exchange," not merely in the same way that he accepted it, as a convenient, because a readily understood, name for a quality, but as expressing the nature of that quality. Thus Adam Smith's explanation of the essential relation of value to the exertion of labor has been virtually, if not utterly, ignored. These succeeding economists have been dissuaded and debarred not only by certain facts not understood, such as the fact that many things having value do not originate in labor, and by erroneous conceptions, such as that which treats labor itself as a commodity; but by a greatly effective recognition of the fact that danger to existing social institutions would follow any too searching an inquiry into the fundamental principle of value. A world of ingenuity has been expended and monstrous books have been written that it will tire a man to read and almost make him doubt his own sanity to try to understand, to solve the problem of the fundamental nature of value in exchange. Yet they have resulted in what are but ponderous elaborations of confusion, for the good and sufficient reason that the essence or foundation of what we call value in exchange does not lie in exchangeability at all, but in something from which exchangeability springs — the toil and trouble attendant upon exertion.

The prevailing theory has been that value is really nothing more than exchangeability. The ingenious and elaborate attempts that have been made to give something like a solid support and logical coherency to this theory have only more clearly shown its utter inadequacy. The latest and most elaborate of these attempts, that of the Austrian or psychological school, is an attempt to emulate in economic reasoning the stories told of East Indian jugglers, who throwing a ball of thread into the air, pull up by it a stouter thread, then a rope, and finally a ladder, on which they ascend until out of sight, and then — come down again!

For whoever will work his way through the perplexities of their reasoning will find that the adherents of this school derive the value of pig-iron, for instance, or even of iron ore in the vein, from the willingness of consumers to pay for higher and more elaborate products into the production of which iron enters, deriving that willingness from a mental estimate on the part of consumers of the utility of those products to them. Thus, as coolly as such stories of Indian jugglers ignore the law of gravitation, do they ignore that law which to political economy is what gravitation is to physics, the law that men seek to satisfy their desires with the least exertion — a law from which proceeds the universal fact that as a matter of exchanging no one will pay more for anything than he is obliged to.

These elaborate attempts to link value on utility, and the utility on individual will or perception, in order to find a support for the idea of value, only show that there is no resting-place in the supposition that value proceeds from exchangeability and can only be relative to other values. The plausibility of this supposition comes from confusion in the use of a simple word.

Exchangeability and Value

Above all words in common use in the English tongue the word "thing" is the widest. It includes whatever may be an object of thought — an atom or a universe; a fact or fancy. But this comprehensiveness of the word we are sometimes apt to forget, or not fully to keep in mind, and to use such phrases as "all things" or "anything" when we really have in mind only things of one particular kind.

When we wish to test the proposition that value is a relation of exchangeability between valuable things, we usually proceed to make a mental experiment with some few valuable things, for it would be impossible to take them all, and tiresome to attempt it. Thus, for instance, we think of money, or as the most widely known representative of money, a piece of gold, and say to ourselves: "Here is a piece of gold. Why is it valuable? It is that it can be exchanged for wheat, hardware, cotton goods and other valuable things. If it could not be so exchanged it would have no value, and the measure of its value is the value of the wheat, hardware, cotton goods and other valuable things for which it is exchangeable. If the relation of exchangeability alters so that for that same piece of gold one can obtain more valuable things, the value of the gold rises, and that of the other valuable things falls." Then, we reverse the standpoint of examination, taking in turn wheat, hardware or cotton goods as representative of a particular instance of value, and gold as representing other valuable things; and seeing that their value depends upon their exchangeable relation in the same way as that of gold in our first experiment, we conclude that value is indeed a relation of exchangeability, and that that is the beginning and end of it.

Thus, that value depends on value, and springs from value and can only be measured by value — seems to us perfectly clear, and we accept the doctrine that there can be no general increase or decrease in values, as if it were but another statement of the axiom that a whole is equal to the sum of its parts, and consequently that all those parts can never be increased or diminished at the same time. The habitual use of money as a common measure of value is apt to prevent any realization of the fact that we are reasoning in a circle.

I think I have correctly described the line of reasoning which makes the derivation of value from exchangeability so plausible. I do not of course mean to say that labor is never taken into account. It is often expressly mentioned and always implied to be one of the valuable things in the category of valuable or exchangeable things. But the weight of the examination is, I think, always thrown upon such things as I have named — things resulting from the exertion of labor; while labor itself is passed over lightly as one of the "other valuable things," and attention never rests upon it.

And, furthermore, I am inclined to think that there always lurks in this examination — which is in reality an examination of the relative value of products of labor — the tacit assumption that the quantity of the valuable things (thought of as products of labor) existing at the specific moment presumed in the examination is a fixed quantity, so that there can be no exchange between those possessed of valuable things (i.e., products of labor) and those possessed of no valuable things (i.e., no products of labor). This, I think, is the case even where the value of labor is given a place in the category of considered values, for what the reputed economists since Smith have called the "value of labor" is in reality the value of the products of labor paid to laborers in wages (which has been usually assumed to come from a fixed quantity, the capital existing at that moment). And on another side, any rigorous examination of the nature of value has been prevented by the universal disposition of economists to slur over the nature of the value of land, and practically to assume, what was indeed the common assumption, that it had the same origin as the value attaching to such things as gold, wheat, hardware, cotton goods or similar products of labor.

That it takes two to make an exchange is clear. But that value in one person's hands does not, as is taught in economic works, necessarily involve the existence of value in the hands of others, may be seen by another imaginative experiment:

Let us imagine some remote and as yet undiscovered island, where men still live as in the Biblical account our first parents lived before the Fall, taking their food from never-failing trees, quenching their thirst from ample and convenient springs, sleeping in the balmy air, without thought of clothing. The power of exerting labor they would of course possess, but of that exertion in itself and of the toil it involves, we may imagine them as ignorant as Adam and Eve in their first estate are supposed to have been. On that island there would clearly be no value. Yet if valuable articles were brought there, would they necessarily lose their value? Could they be parted with only by gift, and would there be no possibility of exchanging them?

Imagine, now, a ship containing such merchandise as would tempt the fancy of a primitive people to come in sight of the island and cast anchor. Would exchange between the ship's people and the Islanders be impossible because of the lack on the part of the Islanders of anything having value? By no means. If nothing else would suffice, the offer of bright cloths and looking-glasses would surely tempt the Eves, if not the Adams; and though never exerted before, the Islanders would exert their power of labor to fill the ship with fruit or nuts or shells, or whatever else of the natural products of the island their exertion could procure, or to pull her on the beach so that she might be caulked, or to fill and roll her water-casks. There was nothing of value on the island before the ship came. Yet the exchanges that would thus take place would be the giving of value in return for value; for on the part of the Islanders value that did not exist before would be brought into existence by the conversion of their labor power through exertion into wealth or services. Even if we suppose the Islanders to relapse into their former easy way of living when their visitors sailed off, there would still remain on the island, where there was no value before, some things having value, and this value would attach to these things until they were destroyed or so long as there remained such desire as would prompt any of the Islanders to render labor in exchange for them. On the other side, the value that the ship would carry off would certainly be not less than the value she contained on arrival, and in all probability would be much more.

Now the way thus illustrated is the way in which the value that attaches to the greater number of valuable things originates. I do not mean it merely to say that this was the way of the first appearance of value among men, but that it is the way in which the value that attaches to what are properly articles of wealth now originates. I do not mean merely to say, as Adam Smith said, that it was "by labor that all the wealth of the world was originally purchased." I mean to say that it is by labor that it is now purchased.

Nothing, indeed, can be clearer than this. Even in the richest of civilized countries, the great body of the people in any civilized society consist of what we call the working class, who live almost literally from hand to mouth, and who have in their possession at any one time little, or practically nothing, of value. Yet they are the purchasers of the great body of articles of value. Where does the value which they thus exchange for value which is already in concrete form come from? Is it not from the conversion of their labor power, through exertion, into value? In common phrase, they exchange their labor for commodities.

How does this fact — the fact that the great body of valuable things pass into the hands of those who have no value to give for them except as they make valuable what before had no value, and are consumed, by being eaten, drunk, burned up or worn out, by them — consort with the theory that value is a relation of exchangeability between valuable things, and that there can be no general increase or decrease of values? Does it not utterly invalidate the theory? Must there not be a constant increase of value to make up for the constant destruction of value, and in spite of it, to permit such growth of aggregate values as we see going on in progressive countries? And in times when the ability to convert labor into values is checked by what we call "want of employment" and great numbers of workers are idle, is there not a clear lessening of the sum of values, a general decrease in values, as compared with the times when there is what we call "abundance of employment," and the great majority of them are at work, turning labor power through exertion into value?

The truth is that current theories of value have resulted from the effort of intelligent men to mold into a semblance of coherency teachings built upon fundamental incoherencies. Let me point out what gives them plausibility, the fallacy involved in the inclusion of labor as "another valuable thing," while the real stress of the examination is laid upon the relative values of such things as gold, wheat, hardware and cotton goods — things that are products of labor. It is a fallacy which our habit of speaking of the buying and selling and exchanging of labor, and our habit of thinking of the value of labor as we think of the value of gold or wheat or hardware or cotton goods, conceals from attention, but which is in reality of fallacy of the kind named by the old logicians "the fallacy of undistributed middle."

Here we come to another instance of the care needed in political economy in the use of words. By the word "labor" we sometimes mean the power of laboring — as when we speak of the exertion of labor, or of labor being employed, or of labor being idle or wasting. Sometimes we mean the act of laboring — as when we speak of the irksomeness or toil of labor. Sometimes we mean the results of laboring — as is the case in most or all of the instances in which we speak of buying, selling or exchanging labor — the real thing bought, sold or exchanged being the results of laboring, that is to say wealth or services. And sometimes, again, we mean the persons who do labor or the persons who have the power and the willingness to labor.

It is clear that labor in the first-mentioned the sense of the word, that of the power or ability of laboring, is not an exchangeable thing and cannot come into any category of values. It resides in the individual body and cannot be taken out of that body and transferred to another, any more than can sight or hearing, or wisdom or courage or skill. I may avail myself of another's skill, courage or wisdom, of his hearing or of his sight, by getting him to exert them for my benefit. And so I may avail myself of another's ability to labor by getting him to do the services, or to produce things which I am to own. But the power of laboring he cannot give, nor I receive. While there are results of its expenditure that may be transferred, the power in itself is intransferable, and therefore unexchangeable.

Now the failure to keep in mind these different senses of the word labor operates to shut off inquiry as to whether the cause of value is not to be found in labor. For since in some senses labor is thought of as having value in exchange, the term, without distinction as to its various senses, is apt to pass in our minds into the category of exchangeable things, with gold or wheat or hardware or cotton goods, and thus the question is unconsciously begged.

But, when we realize that when we say that labor is a valuable thing, we must carefully exclude the sense of labor power, or ability to labor, a confusion is cleared up which has made the search for the true nature of what we call value in exchange a fruitless "swinging round a circle." For since value does not exist in labor power, but does appear where that power takes tangible form through exertion, the fundamental relation of value must be a relation to exertion. But a relation to a exertion in what sense? A relation to exertion positively, or a relation to exertion negatively?

I exchange gold for silver, let us say. In this I give something positively and receive something positively. I get rid of gold and acquire silver. The other party to the exchange gets rid of silver and acquires gold. But when I exchange gold for exertion or toil, do I get rid of gold and acquire toil, and does he get rid of toil and acquire gold? Clearly not. No one wants exertion or toil; all of us want to get rid of it. It is not exertion in a positive sense which is the object of exchange, but exertion in a negative sense; not exertion given or imposed, but exertion avoided or saved. Value, in short, is equivalent to the saving of exertion or toil, and the value of anything is the amount of toil which the possession of that thing will save the possessor, or enable him, to use Adam Smith's phrase, "to impose upon other people" through exchange. Thus, it is not exchangeability that gives value; but value that gives exchangeability. For since it is only by exertion that human desires can be satisfied, whatever will dispense its owner from the toil and trouble of exertion in the satisfaction of desire in that acquires exchangeability.

Let me put the proposition in another form: The current theory is that it is when and because a thing becomes exchangeable that it becomes valuable. My contention is that the truth is just the reverse of this, and it is when and because a thing becomes valuable that it becomes exchangeable.

It is not the toil and trouble which a thing has cost that gives it value. It may have cost much and yet be worth nothing. It may have cost nothing and yet be worth much. It is the toil and trouble that others are now willing, directly or indirectly, to relieve the owner of, in exchange for the thing, by giving him the advantage of the results of exertion, while dispensing him of the toil and trouble that are necessary accompaniments of exertion.

Whether I have obtained a diamond, for instance, by years of hard toil or by merely stooping to pick it up — a movement which can hardly be called an exertion, since it is in itself but a gratification of curiosity which does not involve irksomeness — has nothing whatever to do with its value. That depends upon the amount of toil and trouble that others will undergo for my benefit in exchange for it; or what amounts to the same thing, which they will dispense me of in the satisfaction of my desire, by giving me things in exchange, for which others will undergo toil and trouble.

Desire itself, which is the prompter to exertion, cannot be measured. It is a quantity which, being in its nature subjective, can have no objective measurement until it passes through action into the field of objective existence.

But desire impels to action, as what we call energy or force impels to movement. And while we can no more measure desire in itself than we can measure force in itself, we can measure it in the same way that we measure energy or force — by the resistance it will overcome. Now, while the resistance to movement is inertia, so the resistance to the gratification of desire is the toil and trouble of exertion. It is this that is expressed by and measured in value.

Normally, value and exchangeability are thus always associated and seemingly identical. But in the causal relationship, value comes first. Exchanging is in fact the mutual transfer of value. Of all the qualities of things, value is the only quality of which exchange takes note. Value in exchange, or value in the economic sense, is worth in exertion. It is a quality attaching to the ownership of things, of dispensing with the exertion necessary to secure the satisfaction of desire, by inducing others to take it. Things are valuable in proportion to the amount of exertion which they will command in exchange, and will exchange with each other in that proportion.

The value of a thing in any given time and place is the largest amount of exertion that anyone will render in exchange for it. But as men always seek to gratify their desires with the least exertion this is the lowest amount for which a similar thing can otherwise be obtained.

This of course is not to say that whatever anything may exchange for it is its value. In individual and especially in unaccustomed transactions the point at which any particular exchange takes place may considerably vary. But that our idea of value assumes a normal point, and what this point really is, maybe seen in common speech. Thus we frequently say of the exchange of a certain thing that it brought less than its value, or that it brought more than its value. We say that a thing was exchanged at less than its value because someone else would have given more for it. And so what we deem the point of real value, or actual equivalence, we speak of as market value, from the old idea of the market or meeting place of those who wish to make exchanges, where competition or the higgling both the market brings out of the highest bidding or the lowest offering in transactions of exchange. And when we wish to ascertain the exact value of the thing we offer it at auction or in some other way subject it to competitive offers.

Thus I am justified in saying that the value of a thing in any time and place is the largest amount of exertion that anyone will render in exchange for it; or to make the estimate from the other side, that it is the smallest amount of exertion for which anyone will part with it in exchange.

Chapter 9 — Value of General or Particular Things

Value has of course its origin in the feeling of desire. But the only measure of desire it can afford is akin to the rough and ready way of measuring sorrow which was proposed at a funeral by the man who said: "I am sorry for the widow to the amount of five dollars. How much are the rest of you sorry?" Now, what value determines is not how much a thing is desired, but how much anyone is willing to give for it; not desire in itself, but the desire to possess, accompanied by the ability and willingness to give in return.

Thus it is that there is no measure of value save competition or the higgling of the market, a matter that might be worth the consideration of those amiable reformers who so lightly propose to abolish competition.

It is never the amount of labor that has been inserted in bringing a thing into being that determines its value, but always the amount of labor that will be rendered in exchange for it. Nevertheless, we properly speak of the value of certain things as being determined by their cost of production. But the cost of production that we thus refer to is not the expenditure of labor that has taken place in producing the thing itself, but the expenditure of labor that would now be required to produce a similar thing — not what the thing itself has cost, but what such thing would now cost.

The desire to obtain, which renders men willing to undergo exertion, is, save in rare cases, not the desire for an identical thing, but the desire for a similar thing. Thus, a desire for wheat is not the desire for certain particular grains of wheat; but desire for wheat generally, or wheat of a certain kind.

Thus the point of equation between desire and satisfaction, or as we usually say, between demand and supply, tends in the case of things that can be produced by labor to the cost of production — that is to say, not what the production of the thing has cost, but the present cost of producing a similar thing. Desire remaining, whatever increases the amount of labor that must be expended to obtain similar things by making them will thus tend to increase the value of existing things; and whatever tends to decrease the cost of obtaining similar things by making them will tend to decrease the value of existing things.

But there are some cases in which the desire for a product of labor is not a desire for a similar thing, but for a particular and identical thing. Thus, when that great genius and great toady, Sir Walter Scott, carried off a wine glass from which George IV had drunk, it was to satisfy a desire for that particular glass, which had been honored by the lips of royalty. Where such a desire is felt by only one person (or one economic unit), as where I or my family may value a chair or table or books which once belonged to someone we loved, our valuation does not affect its economic or exchange value, except perhaps as it might make us loath to part with it at its true exchange value. But where more than one person has this desire, which is the case where the possession of a particular article comes to gratify ostentation, it acquires an exchange value which is not limited by the cost of producing a similar thing. Thus, an original picture by a dead master, or an original copy of an old edition of a book, which identically cannot now be produced by any amount of exertion, may have a value not limited by the cost of production. And this may rise to any height to which sentiment or ostentation may carry desire.

The cases I have here taken to illustrate the principle have but small practical application, though they are continually called to attention, and any theory of value must include them. But the principle itself has the widest and most important applications, which steadily increase in importance with the growth of civilization. The value that attaches to land with the growth of civilization is an example of the same principle which governs in the case of a picture by Rafael or Rubens. Land, which in the economic sense includes all the natural opportunities of life, has no cost of production. It was here before man came, and will be here so far as we can see, after he has gone. It is not produced. It was created.

And it was created and still exists in such abundance as even now far to exceed the disposition and power of mankind to use it. Land as land, or land generally — the natural elements necessary to human life and production — has no more value than air as air. But land in special, that is, land of a particular kind or in a particular locality, may have a value such as that which may attach to a particular wine glass or a particular picture or statue; a value which unchecked by the possibility of production has no limit except the strength of the desire to possess it.

This attaching a value to land in special — that is to say, land in particular localities with respect to population — is not merely a most striking feature in the progress of modern civilization, but it is, as I shall hereafter show, the consequence of civilization, lying entirely within the natural order, and furnishing perhaps the most conclusive proof that the intent of that order is the equality of men. Where land is monopolized and the resort of population to unmonopolized landed is shut out either by legal restriction or social conditions, then the desire to use particular land may be based upon the desire to use land generally, or land the natural element; and its strength, measured in the only way in which we can measure the strength of the desire, the willingness to undergo toil and trouble for its gratification, may become, when pushed to full expression, nothing less than the strength of the desire for life itself, for land is the indispensable prerequisite to life, and "all that a man hath he will give for his life."

But in every case the value of land, consisting in the amount of exertion that can be commanded from those who desire to use it by those who have the power of giving or refusing consent to its use, is in the nature of an obligation to render service rather than in that of an exchange of service.

Chapter 10 — The Two Sources of Value

We now come to a point of much importance. For it is from the failure to note what I wish in this chapter to point out that the confusions that have so perplexed the terms of value and wealth in the study of political economy have arisen.

It is usually, if not indeed invariably assumed in all standard economic works that the conversion of labor power through exertion into services or wealth is the only way in which value originates. Yet what we have already seen is enough to show us that this cannot be so. It is not the exertion that a thing has cost, in past time, that gives it value, but the exertion that its possession will in future time dispense with. Thus value may be created by mere agreement to render exertion, or by the imposition of such obstacles to the satisfaction of desire as will necessitate a greater exertion for the attainment of the satisfaction. In the same way, the value of some things may be increased, or sometimes perhaps produced, without the production of real wealth; or even by the destruction of real wealth.

For instance: I with another may agree to exchange, but consummate in the present but one side of the full exchange, substituting for the other side an agreement or obligation to complete it in the future. That is to say, I may give or receive things having present value in return for an obligation to render labor or the results or representatives of labor at some future time. Or, both of us may exchange similar obligations. The obligations thus created may, and frequently do, at once assume value and become exchangeable for exertion or the results of exertion. Or, a government or joint-stock company may issue obligations of the same kind, in the form of bonds or stock, which may at once assume a value dependent as in the case of an individual upon the strength of the belief that the obligations will be faithfully redeemed.

There is in all this no increase of wealth; but there is creation of value — a value arising out of obligation and dependent entirely upon expectations, but still a value — an exchangeable quantity, the possession of which could command through exchange other valuable things.

Now in individual economy, which takes cognizance only of the relations of the individual to other individuals, there is no difference between these two kinds of value. Whether an individual has the power of commanding exertion from others because he has added to the general stock, or simply because he holds the power of demanding exertion from others, makes no difference to him or to them. In either case he gets and they give.

But in political economy, which is the economy of the society or the aggregate, there is a great difference. Value of the one kind — the value which constitutes an addition to the common stock — involves an addition to the wealth of the community or aggregate, and thus is wealth in the politico-economic sense. Value of the other kind — the value which consists merely of the power of one individual to demand exertion from another individual — adds nothing to the common stock. All it effects is a new distribution of what already exists in the common stock, and in the politico-economic sense, is not wealth at all.

In the development of political economy from Adam Smith these two and totally different kinds of values have been confused in one word.

This difficulty might have been avoided in the beginning by giving to the two kinds of values separate names, but the word value has so long been used for both, that the best a science of political economy can do now is to distinguish between value of the one kind and value of the other kind.

This however it is necessary to attempt. The best thing I can do is to distinguish value, not as one, but as of two kinds. By a clear distinction, the various ways in which value may originate, embrace 1) the value which comes from the exertion of labor in such a way as to save the future exertion in obtaining the satisfaction of desire; and, 2) the value which comes from the acquisition of power on the part of some to command or compel exertion on the part of others, or, which is the same thing, from the imposition of obstacles to the satisfaction of desire that render more exertion necessary to the production of the same satisfaction.

Value arising in the first mode may be distinguished as "value from production," and value arising in the second mode may be distinguished as "value from obligation"— for the word obligation is the best word I can think of to express everything which may require the rendering of exertion without the return of exertion.

Value in the sense of exchange value, the only sense in which it can properly be used in political economy, is one and the same quality, just as the water that flows through the outlet of the Nile or Mississippi is one and the same stream. But as we distinguish the sources of these waters as the White Nile and the Blue Nile, or as the Upper Mississippi, the Missouri, the Ohio, etc., so may we distinguish as to origin, between value from production and value from obligation.

The term "value from obligation" will at once be recognized as including an immense body of the values dealt with by banks, stock exchanges, trust companies, or held by private individuals, and which are commonly known as obligations or securities. But it may require a little reflection to see how much else there is having value which is really value from obligation. All debts and claims of whatever kind, all special privileges and franchises, patents, and the beneficial interests known as good will, insofar as they have value, have it as value from obligation. The value of slaves wherever slavery exists — and only a few years ago the market value of slaves in the United States was estimated in round numbers at three thousand million dollars — is clearly a value of obligation, springing not from production, but from the obligation imposed on the slave to work for the master. So too with the value of public pensions and the incumbency of profitable offices and places, when they are made matters of bargain and sale, which is in some cases yet done in England and which is I fear to a still larger extent yet done in the United States, though surreptitiously.

Among the valuable assessments of the larger landholders of feudal times was the right of holding markets, of keeping dovecotes, of succeeding in certain instances to the property of tenants; of grinding grain, of coining money, of collecting floatwood, etc. The values of these were clearly "values from obligation." But that they have passed insensibly into the single right of exacting a rent for the use of land is proof that the value of this right — the right, as it is called, of private ownership of land — is in reality a "value from obligation."

This power to command labor without the return of labor constitutes on the other side an obligation, and it is this that gives it value. Thus a verbal promise, a bank account, a promissory note, or any other instrument of indebtedness, an annuity, an insurance policy, things which frequently have value, derive that value from the fact that they express an obligation to render exertion to the holder or assignee without return. Thus value may be increased sometimes even by the destruction of valuable things, as the Dutch East India Company kept up the value of spices in Europe by destroying great quantities of spices in the islands where they grew; and as our "protective" tariff makes certain things more valuable in the United States than they would otherwise be by imposing fines and penalties on bringing them into the country; or as strikes, as we have recently seen in England and in America, may increase the value of coal or other products; or as a drought, which causes great loss of the corn crop over wide areas, may increase the value of corn, or as a war which lessens the supply of cotton in England may increase the value of cotton there. All such additions to value are "value from obligation," which can no more affect the general stock than can what Jack wins from Tom in a game of cards.

But the most important of these additions to value which do not increase wealth are unquestionably to be found in land value, the form of value from obligation which in the progress of mankind to civilization tends the most rapidly to increase, and which has already in the modern world assumed perhaps more than the relative importance that slavery once held in the ancient world. In an England or a United States, or any other highly civilized country, this importance is already so great that the selling value of the land equals the selling value of all improvements and personal property, while it is the one thing which the natural progress of society, in short all improvements of whatever kind, tend constantly to augment. Yet this value is not part of wealth in the economic sense.

And this is a reason that neither Adam Smith nor those who succeeded him, however much they may have differed as to tweedledum and tweedledee, has realized the true character and dual nature of value. For to recognize that is to come to the conclusion of the Physiocrats that, in the economic sense, land is not wealth. And this involves a revolution, a beneficent revolution, greater than the world has yet seen.

Yet it is perfectly clear. Let us go back in thought to our imaginary Isle of Eden, and suppose that its discoverers, instead of making merchandise of the inhabitants themselves, had done at once what the American missionaries did gradually in the

Hawaiian Islands — made themselves owners of the island, and with power to enforce their claim by punishment, had forbidden any islander to pluck of a tree or drink of a spring without their permission. Land before valueless would at once become valuable, for the Islanders, having nothing else to give, would be compelled to render exertion, or the products of exertion, for the privilege of continuing in life.

"The value of the thing is just what you can get for it," is a saying, current among men who have never bothered their heads with political economy, which concisely expresses the conception of value. A thing has no value if nothing can be got in exchange for it, and it has value when, so long as, and to the degree that, it may be exchanged for some other thing or things.

But all things having value cannot be exchanged for all other things having value. I could not for instance, exchange a million dollars' worth of cheesecakes for a building worth a million dollars. What then is the one thing for which all things having value must directly or indirectly exchange? We are apt to ignore that question, because we habitually think of value in terms of money, which serves us as a flux for the exchange of all values. But if we press the question, we see that everything having value must ultimately be exchangeable into human exertion, and that it is in this that its value consists. There are some valuable things that cannot readily, and some that it is practically impossible to exchange for exertion — such, for instance, as an equatorial telescope, a locomotive, a steamship, a promissory note or bond of large amount, or a bank-note or greenback of high denomination. But they derive their value from the fact that they can be exchanged for things that can in turn be exchanged for exertion.

Money itself derives its power of serving as a medium or flux of exchanges from the fact that it is of all things that which is most readily exchangeable for exertion, and it utterly loses value when it ceases to be exchangeable for exertion. This we have seen in the United States in the case of the Continental currency, in the case of the notes of broken State banks and in the case of the Confederate currency. Thus value ends as it begins, with the power of commanding exertion, and is always measured by that power.

Value in the economic sense is not a mere relation of exchangeability between valuable things, which, save relatively, as between one particular thing and another particular thing, can neither increase nor diminish. The real relation of value is with human exertion, or rather with the toil and trouble that are the inseparable adjuncts of exertion; and the true and absolute value of anything, that which makes it comparable with that of any or all other things in all times and places, is the difficulty or ease of acquiring it. That is of high value which is hard to get; that is of low value which is easy to get; while that which may be had without exertion, and that which no one will undergo exertion to get, has no value at all. Cheapness or low value means that the satisfactions of desire may be obtained with little effort, dearness or high value means that they can be obtained only with much effort. Thus there may be general increase or decrease of value as clearly and as truly as there may be general scarcity or general abundance.

The recognition of this simple theory of value will enable us as we proceed to clear up, with ease and certainty, many points which have perplexed the economists who have ignored it, and are to their students stumbling-blocks, which make them doubt whether any real science of political economy is possible. In its light all the complex phenomena of value and exchange become clear, and are seen to be but illustrations of that fundamental law of the human mind which impels men to seek the gratification of their desires with the least exertion.

Whatever increases the obstacles, natural or artificial, to the gratification of desire on the part of the ultimate users or consumers of things, thus compelling them to expend more exertion or undergo more toil and trouble to obtain those things, increases their value; whatever lessens the exertion that must be expended, decreases value. Thus, wars, tariffs, pirates, public insecurity, monopolies, taxes and restrictions of all kinds, which render more difficult the satisfaction of the desire for certain things, increase their value, and discoveries, inventions and improvements which lessen the exertion required for bringing things to the satisfaction of desire, lessen their value.

Here we may see at once the clear solution of the question which has perplexed and still perplexes many minds — the question whether the artificial increase of values by governmental restriction is or is not in the interest of the community. When we regard value as a simple relation of exchangeability between exchangeable things, there may seem room for debate. But when we see that its relation is to the toil and trouble which must be undergone by ultimate users in the satisfaction of desire, there is no room for debate. Scarcity may be at times to the relative interest of the few, but abundance is always to the general interest.

Chapter 11 — The Meaning of Wealth in Political Economy

We are now in a position to fix the meaning of wealth as an economic term. The confusion into which, after more than a hundred years of cultivation, the teaching of political economy has fallen as to the meaning of its principal term is clearly due to confusion as to the meaning of the term value. The scholastic development of political economy since Adam Smith has tended to cover up the vital distinction between the two sources of value in exchange; that originating in the storing up of labor, and that originating in what I have called obligation — the power, often devoid of moral right, to compel the expenditure of labor.

This is the condition in which the orthodox political economy now is. It has not only not discovered what its principal term, wealth in the economic sense, really is, but it has so confounded other terms as to give little light on the search.

Value from production, which is the only kind of value which gives wealth, consists in application of labor in the production of wealth which adds to the common stock of wealth. Wealth, therefore, in political economy consists in natural products so secured, moved, combined or altered by human labor as to fit them for human satisfaction. Value from obligation, on the other hand, though a most important element of value, does not result in increase in the common stock, or in the production of wealth. It has nothing whatever to do with the production of wealth, but only with the distribution of wealth, and its proper place is under that heading.

As there is a reason for everything, in the mental world as truly as in the physical world, so there is a reason for the disposition to include in the term wealth everything that has value, without regard to the origin of that value. It springs at bottom from the desire on the part of those who dominate the accredited organs of education and opinion (who wherever there is inequality in the distribution of wealth are necessarily the wealthy class) to give to the mere legal right of property the same moral sanction that justly attaches to the natural right of property, or at the very least to ignore anything that would show that the recognition of a legal right may involve the denial of a moral right. As the defenders of chattel slavery, and those who did not wish to offend the slave power, not long since dominant in the United States, were obliged to stop their examination of ownership with purchase, assuming that the purchase of a slave carried with it the same right of ownership as did the purchase of a mule or of a bale of cotton, so those who would defend the industrial slavery of today are obliged to stop their examination of the nature of wealth with value, assuming that everything that has value is therefore wealth, thus involving themselves and leaving their students in a fog of confusion as to the nature of the thing whose laws they profess to examine.

As commonly used the word wealth, when applied to the possessions of an individual, includes all purchasing power, and is indeed in most cases synonymous with exchange value. But this use of the word is really representative, like the similar use we make of the word money. We say that a man has so much money, without meaning that he has in his possession so much actual money. We mean only that he has what would exchange for so much money. Such representative use of the word money or of the terms of money does not, in everyday affairs, in the least confuse us as to the real meaning of the word. If asked to explain what money is, no one would think of saying that sheep and ships, and lands and houses are money, although he is in the constant habit of speaking of their possession as the possession of money.

So it is with the common use of the word wealth. In the economy of individuals, to which our ordinary speech usually refers, the word wealth is commonly applied to anything having an exchange value as between individuals. But when used as a term of political economy the word wealth must be limited to a much more definite meaning. Many things are commonly spoken of as wealth in the hands of the individual, which in taking account of collective or general wealth cannot be included. Such things are not really wealth, inasmuch as their increase or decrease does not affect the sum of wealth. Such are bonds, mortgages, promissory notes, or other stipulations for the transfer of wealth. Such are franchises, which represent special privileges, accorded to sum and denied to others. Such were slaves, whose value represented merely the power of one class to appropriate the earnings of another class. Such are lands or other natural opportunities, the value of which results from the acknowledgment in favor of certain persons of an exclusive legal right to their use, and the profit of their use. Increase in the value of bonds, mortgages, notes or bank-bills cannot increase the wealth of a community that includes those who promise to pay as well as those who are entitled to receive. Increase in land values does not represent increase in the common wealth, for what landowners gain by higher prices the tenants, or ultimate users, who must pay them, are deprived of. And all this value which, in common thought and speech, in legislation and law, is undistinguished from wealth, could, without the destruction or consumption of anything more than a few drops of ink and a piece of paper, be utterly annihilated. By enactment of the sovereign political power debts might be canceled, franchises abolished or taken by the state, slaves emancipated, and land returned to the general usufructuary ownership of the whole people, without the aggregate wealth being diminished by the value of a pinch of snuff, for what some would lose others would gain. There would be no more destruction of wealth than there was creation of wealth when Elizabeth Tudor enriched her favorite courtiers by the grant of monopolies, or when Boris Godoonof made Russian peasants into merchantable property.

All articles of wealth have value. If they lose value, they cease to be wealth. But all things having value are not wealth, as is erroneously taught in current economic works. Only such things can be wealth the production of which increases and the destruction of which decreases the aggregate of wealth. If we consider what these things are, and what their nature is, we shall have no difficulty in defining wealth.

When we speak of a community increasing in wealth — as when we say that England has increased in wealth since the accession of Victoria, or that California is now a wealthier country than when it was a Mexican territory — we do not mean to say that there is more land, or that the natural powers of the land are greater, for the land is the same and its natural powers are the same. Nor yet do we mean that there are more people in the same area, for when we wish to express that idea we speak of increase of population. Nor yet do we mean that the debts or dues owed by some of these people to others of their number have increased. But we mean that there is an increase of certain tangible things, having a value that comes from production, such as buildings, cattle, tools, machinery, agricultural and mineral products, manufactured goods, ships, wagons, furniture and the like. The increase of such things is an increase of wealth; their decrease is a lessening of wealth; and the community that, in proportion to its numbers, has the most of such things is the wealthiest community.

Thus, wealth, as alone the term can be used in political economy, consists of labor impressed upon matter in such a way as to store up, as the heat of the sun is stored up in coal, its power to minister to human desires. Nothing that nature supplies to man without the expenditure of labor is wealth; nor yet does the expenditure of labor result in wealth unless there is a tangible product which retains the power of ministering to desire; nor yet again can man himself, nor any of his powers or capabilities, nor any obligation to bestow labor or yield up the products of labor from one to another, constitute any part of wealth. Nature and man — or, in economic terminology, land and labor — are the two necessary factors in the production of wealth. Wealth is the result of their joint action.

And though Adam Smith nowhere formally defined wealth, being mainly occupied with showing that it did not consist exclusively in money or the precious metals; and though incidentally he fell into confusion in regard to it, yet, as may be seen from the passages in the *Wealth of Nations* before quoted, this was his idea of wealth when he came to look at it directly — the idea of products of labor, still retaining the power, impressed upon them by labor, of ministering to human desire.

Now in our common use of the word wealth we make no distinction between the various kinds of things that have value, as to the origin of that value, but class them all together under the one word, wealth, speaking of the sum of value which an individual may have at his command as his wealth, or sometimes as his money. This metaphorical use of words is so embedded in common speech that it would be hopeless to object to it in common usage.

Chapter 12 — The Genesis of Wealth

It is so all-important that we should know precisely and certainly just what the chief factor of political economy, wealth, is, so that we may hereafter be in no doubt whatever about it but may confidently reason from our knowledge of its nature, that I propose to reinforce all that has been said by showing just how wealth originates and what in essence it actually is.

Wealth is a result of human exertion. But all human exertion does not result in wealth. Not merely is there failure and misadventure in the application of effort to the production of wealth, but the production of wealth is not the only purpose of human effort. All human actions proceed from desire and have their aim and end in the satisfaction of desire. But if we consider those actions of man which aim at material satisfactions, we see that there is a distinction as to the way in which satisfaction is sought. In some the satisfaction sought is direct and immediate. In others it is indirect and delayed.

To put myself in imagination in the position of my most remote ancestor: I am moved by the desire we call hunger or appetite, or it is aroused in me by the sight of a tree laden with fruit. I pluck and eat the fruit, and I am satisfied. Or I feel the desire called thirst, and a stooping down to a spring, I drink, and am again satisfied. Action and satisfaction are in such cases confined to the same person, and the connection between them is direct and immediate. Or, my wife is with me. She feels the same desires; but is not tall enough to pluck the fruit and cannot as well climb a tree or so readily stoop to the spring. So, I pluck the fruit that she may eat, and hollowing my hands give her to drink.

These are the ways in which in nearly all cases the animals satisfy their desires. There is nothing in their actions which goes beyond the direct and immediate satisfaction of desire. The cow that has browsed all day or the bird that has brought worms to her young has done nothing towards the satisfaction of desire that will recur tomorrow.

In such cases there is no suggestion of anything we would call wealth. And in a world where all human desires were satisfied in this direct and immediate way there would be no wealth, no matter how great the activities of man or how abundant the spontaneous offerings of nature for the satisfaction of his desires.

But man is a reasoning being, who looks beyond the immediate promptings of desire, and who adapts means to ends. An animal would merely eat of the fruit or drink of the spring to the full satisfaction of present desire. But the man might, after satisfying his immediate desire, carry off with him some of the fruit to ensure a like satisfaction on the morrow, or with a still longer prevision plant its kernel with a view to satisfaction in future years. Or with a view to the future satisfaction of thirst, he might enlarge the spring or scoop out a vessel in which to carry water, or dig a channel or construct a pipe. In such cases action would be spent not in the direct and immediate satisfaction of desire, but in the doing of what might indirectly and in the future aid in satisfying desire.

The essential character of wealth is that of the embodiment or storage in material form of action aiming at the satisfaction of desire, so that this action obtains a certain permanence — a capability of remaining for a time as at a stopping-place, whence it may be taken, either to yield satisfaction to desire, or to be carried forward towards the satisfaction of desire requiring yet more effort.

Thus, for the satisfaction of desire by the eating of bread, effort must first be expended to grow the grain; then to harvest it; and then to grind it into flour; then to bake the flour into bread. At each of these stages there is an increment of wealth: that is to say, some part of the effort required to reach the point of yielding the final satisfaction has been accomplished, and is tied or stored in concrete form, so that what has been gained towards the final result may be utilized in the remaining stages of the process. Grain is an article of wealth expressing the effort necessary in growing and harvesting, in such form that it may be from thence carried forward to the satisfaction of desire, either by feeding it to domestic animals, converting it into starch or alcohol etc., or by turning it into flour and making bread. Flour again is an article of wealth embodying the effort necessary to the production of grain and the further effort required in grinding; and bread an article of wealth embodying that and the additional effort required in baking, in a form in which consumption will give the satisfaction to desire of which bread is capable.

The idea of wealth cannot be reduced to that of satisfaction, since even when the intent and the result of the effort is a satisfaction of the desire on the part of the expender of the effort, there is necessarily an intermediate step, in which the expended effort pauses or is stored up for an interval in concrete form, and whence it may be released not merely to satisfy the desire of the expender of the effort, but that of another as well. If I pluck fruit today for the satisfaction of tomorrow's appetite, the satisfaction I then obtained when eating it would not be to me the direct result of an effort, but would yield me satisfaction as a result of a service — a service of which I myself would be the direct beneficiary, but still no less truly a service than it would be in the case of my wife were she the recipient of the satisfaction.

Thus if we wish to bring the idea of wealth into a larger generalization, the term of widest inclusiveness that we could select would be a word which would express the idea of service without limitation as to mode. The essential idea of wealth is really that of service embodied in material form, and all our enjoying of wealth, or exchanging of wealth, or giving of wealth, or updating of wealth, is really at bottom the adjoining or exchanging or giving or updating of service, a word which involves the possibility of distinction in person between the exerter of effort and the recipient of the final satisfaction, which is its aim.

In the first and simplest form of service, that in which the recipient gets directly the satisfaction brought about by the action (and to which for the sake of distinction the term service should be reserved), though it is capable of being given, received and exchanged, is so capable only within very narrow limits, since the action is spent in such direct service and is over and done, whereas in action resulting in wealth the action is not spent, but is stored in intermediate and material form, to be spent in gratification when required. In direct service the power of human action to satisfy human desire is like the exertion of the power of electricity in the lightning-flash. But in indirect service, through the medium of wealth, the action remains unused for a time in readily exchangeable form, whence it may be called forth for use, as the power of electricity remains in transportable and exchangeable form in the storage battery.

I may black your boots with the understanding that you shall in return shave my face, or gratify you by telling a story on condition that you shall gratify me by singing a song, and the possibilities of such exchange may be somewhat widened by the understanding that though I black your boots or tell you the story today, you may give me the shave or sing the song at a future time, and do this either for me or for anyone whom I may present to receive in my place the promised service. But manifestly the exchange of services that may take place in that way is as nothing compared with the exchange that becomes possible when service is embodied in concrete form and wealth and may be passed from hand to hand and used at will in the satisfaction of desire.

By this transmutation of labor into wealth the exchange even of such services as cannot be transmuted into wealth, since they must be rendered directly to the person, is much facilitated. I desire, for instance, such service from another as the carrying of a bag or message, or the conveyance of myself and my luggage from one place to another by cab or train. There is no equivalent service on my part desired by those whose services I wish, but by the intervention of wealth the satisfaction of desire on both sides becomes possible, and the exchange is completed there and then; those from whom I obtain the service receiving from me some article of wealth or representative of wealth which they can in turn exchange either for wealth or for direct services from others. It is thus, and only thus, that the great body of exchanges of direct services that take place in civilization becomes possible. Indeed, without wealth it is difficult to see how men could avail themselves of one another's powers to a much greater extent than do the animals; for that some animals exchange services, whoever has watched monkeys reciprocally ridding each other of fleas must have realized.

The essential idea of wealth being that of exertion impressed on matter, or the power of rendering services stored in concrete form, to talk of immaterial wealth, as some professed economists now talk, is as much a contradiction in terms as it would be to talk of square circles or triangular squares. Nothing can really be an object of wealth that is not tangible to the senses. Nor in the strictest sense of the term, can wealth include any natural substance, or form, or power, unmodified by man's exertion, nor any human power or capacity of exertion. To talk of natural wealth, or to talk of human skill, knowledge or energy as included in wealth is also a contradiction in terms.

Chapter 13 — The Wealth That is Called Capital

That part of wealth devoted to the production of other wealth is what is properly called capital. Capital is not a different thing from wealth. It is but part of wealth, differing from other wealth only in its use, which is not directly to satisfy desire, but indirectly to satisfy desire by associating in the production of other wealth.

To return to the simplest illustration given in the last chapter: the man who, finding a fruit tree, plucks and eats, expends labor in the most direct and primitive form, that of satisfying desire. His desire is for the moment satisfied, but the labor he has exerted is all spent; no result remains which will help to the future satisfaction of desire.

But if, not content with a satisfaction of present desire, he carries off some of the fruit to where he may in the future more conveniently obtain it, he has in this gathered fruit a concrete result of the expenditure of labor. His labor expended in the gathering and removal of the fruit which he retains has been as it were stored up, as energy may be stored up by bending a bow or raising a stone, to be utilized again at a future time. This stored-up labor, concretely in this case — this gathered and transported fruit — is wealth, and will retain this character of wealth or stored-up labor, until it is 1) consumed, by being applied to the gratification of desire; or 2) destroyed, as by decay, or the ravages of insects or animals.

But the man who has thus obtained the possession of wealth by gathering fruit and carrying it to a more convenient place may utilize its potency of ministering to desire in different ways. Let us suppose him to divide this wealth, this gathered fruit, into three portions. One portion he will eat as he feels desire; another portion he will give to some other man in exchange for some other form of wealth; and the third portion he will plant in order that in the future he may more readily and more abundantly satisfy his desire for such fruit.

All three of these portions are alike wealth. But the first portion is merely wealth; its use is the final use of all wealth — the satisfaction of desire. But the second and third portions are not simply wealth — they are capital. Their use is in obtaining more or other wealth, which in its turn may be used for the satisfaction of desire.

By the storage of labor, which is involved in the production of wealth, it becomes possible for man to change the time in which a given exertion shall be utilized in the satisfaction of desire, thus greatly increasing the sum of satisfactions which a given exertion may procure. And by the using of wealth as capital, which is the calling of past exertion to the service of present exertion, he is enabled to concentrate exertion upon a given point, at a given time, to call in, as it were, forces of nature which far transcend in their power those which nature has put at his use in the human frame.

To illustrate: nature gives to the bull in his massive skull and sharp horns a weapon of offense by which almost the whole strength of his frame may be concentrated upon one or two narrow points, thus utilizing the maximum of force upon the minimum of resistance. She has given to man no such weapon, for his clenched fist, the nearest approach to the horns of the bull his bodily resources furnish, is a far inferior weapon. But by turning his labor into capital in the shape of a spear he is enabled on occasion to concentrate nearly the whole force of his body upon an even narrower point than can the bull; and by turning labor into capital in the form of a bow, he may exert in one instant the force that can be accumulated during longer intervals of time; and finally, as a result of many transmutations of labor into capital, he can exert in the rifle chemical forces more potent than any of the forces of which the energies of his own body give him command.

It is likewise to be observed that the term capital is subject to all the restrictions and limitations that apply to the term wealth. Personal qualities such as knowledge, skill or industry are qualities of labor and can never be properly treated as capital. While in common speech it may be permissible to speak in a metaphorical sense of such qualities as capital, meaning thereby that they are susceptible of yielding to their possessors advantages akin to the advantages given by capital, yet to transfer this metaphorical use of speech to economic reasoning is, as many ponderous treatises will testify, provocative of fundamental confusion.

To recur to our first simple illustration: a high chief of the Hawaiian Islands might, on discovering a tree laden with fruit, have eaten his fill and then laid the tree under Taboo. He might thus have obtained for himself something of the same advantages that he would have obtained by carrying some of the fruit to a more convenient place. The inhibition upon others might have led some of them, in return for the privilege of taking it, to consent to bring him some. But the result would not have been the same to the community as a whole. His Laziness could have obtained the fruits of labor, but only by virtually taking the labor of others.

Chapter 14 — Why Political Economy Considers Only Wealth

Political economy has been defined, and I think sufficiently, as "the science which treats of the nature of wealth and the laws of its production and distribution." The object-noun or subject-matter of political economy is therefore wealth. Now, as we have already seen, wealth is not the only result of human exertion, nor is it indeed the final cause of human exertion. That is not reached until wealth is spent or consumed in satisfaction of desire. Wealth itself is in fact only a halting-place or storehouse on the way between prompting desire and final satisfaction; a point at which exertion, journeying towards the satisfaction of desire, remains for a time stored up in concrete form, and from whence it may be called forth to yield the satisfaction which is its ultimate aim. And there are exertions aiming at the satisfaction of desire which do not pass through the form of wealth at all.

Why then should political economy concern itself merely with the production and distribution of wealth? Is not the proper object of the science the production and distribution of human satisfactions, and would not this definition, while including wealth, as material satisfactions through material services, also include services that do not take concrete form? My answer is that a consideration of the production and distribution of wealth will include all that there is any practical use of considering of the production and distribution of satisfactions. While wealth does not include the sum of all exertions for the satisfaction of material desires, it does include what in a highly civilized society are the far greater part of them, and is, as it were, the exchange point or clearing-house where the transfer of services devoted not to the production of wealth, but to the direct procurement of satisfactions, is made.

The barber, the singer, the physician, and the actor do not produce wealth, but direct satisfactions. But not only are their efforts which are expended in this way mainly devoted to the procurement of wealth, which they get in exchange for their services, but any exchange between themselves of services for services takes place through the medium of wealth. To this we may add that the laws which govern the production and distribution of services are essentially the same as those which govern the production and distribution of wealth. Thus we see that all the ends of political economy may be reached if its inquiry be an inquiry into the nature of wealth and the laws that govern its production and distribution.

Political economy has a duty and a province of its own. It is not and it cannot be the science of everything; for the day in which any one scheme can include the whole province of human knowledge has long past, and must with the increase of human knowledge further recede. Even today the science of politics, though closely related, is, as I conceive it, clearly distinct from the science of political economy, to say nothing of the almost numberless other schemes which treat of man's relations to other individuals and to the relations with which he is brought in contact.

Chapter 15 — Moral Confusions as to Wealth

As to the desire for wealth in the politico-economic sense, as I have described it, there is nothing sordid or mean. Wealth, on the contrary, is a perfectly legitimate object of desire and effort. To obtain it is simply to increase the powers of the individual over nature, and is prompted by the same essentially noble desire as in any way to increase our powers or our knowledge, or in any way to raise ourselves above the level of the mere animal, from which we start; while no one can increase his own wealth by increasing value from production, without at the same time doing something for everyone else.

How then is it that wealth is so widely regarded askance by our moral perceptions; that we are told that we should not seek it, and hardly even use it; that the highest expressions of our deepest knowledge look at it so contemptuously, and that political economy, which is the science of the nature, production and exchange of wealth, should be so widely regarded as a selfish and hard science? If we go into this question at all we must go deeper than has yet, I think, been done.

There is a distinction on which our examination of wealth and value may throw light, the distinction we commonly make between the rich and the poor. We mean by a rich man a man who has much that has value, that is to say, much wealth or much power of commanding wealth or services from others. And by a poor man we mean a man who possesses little or nothing of such value. But where is the line of division between rich and poor? There is no line distinctly recognized in common thought, and a man is called rich or poor according to the standard of average comfort prevailing in the society or rather the grade of society in which the estimate is made. There are circles of human life in New York City in which no man would be deemed poor who could see his way to a night's lodging and breakfast in the morning, and there are other circles in which a Vanderbilt could say that a man possessed of only $1 million could with economy live as comfortably as though he were rich.

But is there not some line the recognition of which will enable us to say with something like scientific precision that this man is rich and that man is poor? It seems to me that there must be. And if we stop to think of it, we may see that there is.

If we set aside for the moment the narrower economic meaning of service (by which direct service is conveniently distinguished from the indirect service embodied in wealth), we may resolve all the things which indirectly satisfy human desire into one term, service; just as we resolve fractions into a common denominator. Now, is there not a natural or normal line of the possession or enjoyment of service? Clearly there is. It is that of equality between giving and receiving. This is the equilibrium which Confucius expressed in the golden word of his teaching that in English we translate into "reciprocity." Naturally the services which a member of human society is entitled to receive from other members are the equivalents of those he renders to others. Here is a normal line from which what we call wealthiness and what we call poverty take their start. He who can command more service then he need render, is rich. He is poor, who can command less service that he does render or is willing to render; for in our civilization of today we must take note of the monstrous fact that men willing to work cannot always find opportunity to work. Rich and poor are thus correlatives of each other — the existence of a class of rich involving the existence of a class of poor, and the reverse. Abnormal luxury on the one side and abnormal want on the other have a relation of necessary sequence. To put this relation into terms of morals, the rich are the robbers, since they are at least sharers in the proceeds of robbery; and the poor are the robbed.

This is the reason, I take it, why Christ, who was not really a man of such reckless speech as some Christians deem Him to have been, always expressed sympathy with the poor and repugnance of the rich. In His philosophy it was better even to be robbed than to rob. In the kingdom of right-doing which He preached, rich and poor would be impossible, because rich and poor in the true sense are the results of wrongdoing. And when He said, "it is easier for a camel to pass through the eye of the needle than for a rich man to enter the kingdom of heaven!" He simply put in the emphatic forms of Eastern metaphor a statement of fact as coldly true as the statement that two parallel lines can never meet.

Injustice cannot live where justice rules, and so it is utterly impossible in this, or in any other conceivable world, to abolish unjust poverty, without at the same time abolishing unjust possessions. This is a hard word to the softly amiable philanthropists who, to speak metaphorically, would like to get on the good side of God without angering the devil. But it is a true word nevertheless.

Chapter 16 — The Permanence of Wealth

Wealth consists of material things. These things are taken, as it were, by labor from the reservoirs of nature, and by virtue of their materiality tend back to those reservoirs again from the moment they are taken, just as water, taken from the ocean, tends back to the ocean. The great body of wealth is, indeed, produced for immediate consumption. Even the parts not subject to immediate destruction are subject to destruction by the action of the elements, by mechanical and chemical disintegration, and finally by being lost. Indeed, the far greater part of material things, if not absolutely all of them, after they have been brought into existence, require the constant exertion of labor to keep them in existence and prevent their relapsing into nature's reservoirs again.

But things having a value which does not come from the exertion of labor and which represents only the power given by human law, agreement or custom of appropriating the proceeds of exertion, have their real existence in the human mind. The papers which we use in transferring them or proclaiming them are not the things themselves, but merely aids to memory. The essence of a debt is not the due-bill or promissory note, but a moral obligation or mental agreement; the essence of a franchise is not the written charter or engrossed act of legislature, but the will of the sovereign, theoretically supposed to be the will of all; the ownership of land is not in the title-deeds, but in the same sovereign will or supposed general agreement.

Now, the values which cannot be included in the category of wealth are as a class much more enduring than the values which are properly so included. We of the modern civilization generally limit the time during which debts, promissory notes, and similar obligations of the individual can be legally enforced. But there are devices by which a value which is in reality but an obligation to render future labor may be continued for longer periods; while many values of similar nature we treat as perpetual, as is the case with public debts, with some franchises, and with exclusive rights to land. These may retain their value unimpaired, while the value of the great body of articles of wealth lessens and disappears.

How little of the wealth in existence in England two hundred years ago exists now! And the infinitesimal part that still exists has been maintained in existence only by constant care and toil. But stock in the public debt of England incurred then still retains value. So do perpetual pensions granted to their favorites by English kings long dust. These things have cost no care or trouble to maintain. On the contrary, they have been sources of continual revenue to their owners — have enabled their owners to call continually upon generation after generation to undergo toil and trouble for their benefit. Yet their value, that is to say their power of continuing to do this, remains still, not merely unimpaired, but in many cases enormously increased.

So far as we can see with any certainty, the quality of value has longer and more constantly attached to the ownership of land, which is not an article of wealth, than to any other valuable thing. The little piece of land in the Sabine hills, which Mæcenas gave to Horace, had doubtless been bought and sold and exchanged for centuries before that, and has, I doubt not, a value to this day. It is this permanence of value which has led the lawyers to distinguish property in land, though it is not wealth at all, as real estate or real property. Its value remains so long as population continues around it and custom or municipal law guarantees a special privilege of appropriating the profits of its use.

And between articles of wealth and things of the nature of special privileges, like franchises and property in land, which though having value are not wealth, there is still another very important distinction to be noted. The general tendency of the value attached to the one is to decrease and disappear with social advance. The general tendency of the value attaching to the other is to increase.

For social advance, involving, as it does, increase of population, extensions of exchange and improvement of the arts, tends constantly, by lessening the cost of production, steadily to reduce the value of the great body of articles of wealth already in existence. The value of almost all the products of labor has been of late years steadily and largely reduced in this way, while the value of much costly machinery has been and still is being destroyed by discoveries, inventions and improvements, which render their use in production antiquated. But the growth of population and the augmentations of the productive power of labor increase enormously the value of such special privileges as franchises and land ownership in the highways and centers of social life.

It will be seen from our analysis, as indeed from observation, that the amount of wealth at any time existing is very much less than is usually assumed. The vast majority of mankind live not on stored wealth, but on their exertion. The vast majority of mankind, even in richest civilized countries, leave the world as destitute of wealth as they entered it. It is the constant expenditure of labor that alone keeps up the supply of wealth. If labor were to cease, wealth would disappear.

Part III — The Production of Wealth

Chapter 1 — The Meaning of Production

The word production comes from the Latin, *pro,* before, and *ducere,* to draw, and its literal meaning is a drawing forth.

Production, as a term of political economy, means a drawing forth by man; a bringing into existence by the power of man. It does not mean creation, the proper sense of which is a bringing into existence by a power superior to that of man. Nothing that is created can in the politico-economic sense be said to be produced. Man is not a creator; he has no power of originating things, of making something out of nothing. He is a producer; that is to say a changer, who brings forth by altering what already is. All his making of things, his causing things to be, is a drawing forth, a modification in place or relation, and in accordance with natural laws, which he neither originated nor altered, of what he finds already in existence. All his production has as its substratum what he finds already in the world; what exists irrespective of him. This substratum or nexus, the natural or passive factor, on which and by which the human or active factor of production acts, is in the terminology of political economy called land.

In common speech, the word production is frequently used in a sense which distinguishes the first from the later stages of wealth-getting; and those engaged in the primary extractive or formative processes are often styled producers, as distinguished from transporters or exchangers. This use of the word production may be convenient where we wish to distinguish between separable functions, but we must be careful not to import it into our use of the economic term. In the economic meaning of the word production, the transporter or exchanger, or anyone engaged in any sub-division of those functions, is as truly engaged in production as is the primary extractor or maker. A newspaper-carrier or the keeper of a newsstand would for instance in common speech be styled a distributor. But in economic terminology he is not a distributor of wealth, but a producer of wealth. Although his part in the process of producing the newspaper comes last, not first, he is as much a producer as the paper-maker or type-founder, the editor or compositor or press-man.

For the object of production is the satisfaction of human desires, that is to say it is consumption; and this object is not made capable of attainment, that is to say, production is not really complete, until wealth is brought to the place where it is to be consumed and put at the disposal of him whose desire it is to satisfy.

Thus, the production of wealth in political economy includes transportation and exchange. The distribution of wealth, on the other hand, has in economic phraseology no relation to transportation or exchange, but refers, as we shall see when we come to treat of it, to the division of the results of production. This fact has been ignored by the great majority of professed economists who with few exceptions treat of exchange under the heading of the distribution of wealth instead of giving it its proper place under the heading of the production of wealth.

Chapter 2 — The Three Modes of Production

All production results from human exertion upon external nature, and consists in the changing in place, condition, form or combination of natural materials or objects so as to fit them or more nearly fit them for the satisfaction of human desires.

But production takes place in different ways. If we run over in mind as many examples as we can think of in which the exertion of labor results in wealth — either in those primary or extractive stages of production in which what before was not wealth is made to assume the character of wealth; or in the later or secondary stages, in which an additional value or increment of wealth is attached to what has already been given the character of wealth — we find that they fall into three categories or modes.

The first of these three modes of production, for both reason and tradition unite in giving it priority, is the mode of production of the fisherman, the hunter, the miner, the smelter, the refiner, the manufacturer. We use it when we produce wealth by taking coal from the vein and changing its place to the surface of the earth; and again when we bring about a further increment of wealth by carrying the coal to the place where it is to be consumed in the satisfaction of human desires. We use this mode of production when we convert trees into lumber, or lumber into boards; when we convert wheat into flour, or the juice of the cane or beet into sugar; when we separate the metals from the combinations in which they are found in the ores, and when we unite them in new combinations that give us desirable alloys such as brass or bronze, or when by the various processes of separating and recombining we produce the textile fabrics, and convert them again into clothes, or when by bringing their various materials into suitable forms and combinations, we construct tools, machines, or houses. In fact, all that in the narrower sense we usually call "manufacturing" is brought about by the application of labor in this first mode of production — the mode of "adapting."

In the Northwest, however, they speak sometimes of "manufacturing wheat;" in the West of "making hogs," and in the South of "making cotton" (the fiber) or "making tobacco" (the leaf). But in such local or special senses the words manufacturing or making are used as equivalent to producing. The sense is not the same, nor is the suggested action in the same mode, as when we properly speak of flour as being manufactured, or of bacon, cotton cloth or cigars being made. Wonderful machines are indeed constructed by man's power of adaptation. But no extension of his power of adaptation will enable him to construct a machine that will feed itself and produce its kind. His power of adapting extended infinitely would not enable him to manufacture a single wheat grain that would sprout, or to make a hog or a cotton-boll. The tiniest of such things are as much above man's power of adapting as is the "making" of a world or the "manufacture" of the solar system.

There is, however, another or second mode of production. In this man utilizes the vital or reproductive forces of nature to aid him in producing wealth. By obtaining vegetables, cuttings or seeds, and planting them; by capturing animals and breeding them, we are enabled not merely to produce vegetables and animals in greater quantity than Nature spontaneously offers them to our taking, but in many cases, to improve their quality of adaptability to our uses. This second mode of production, the mode in which we make use of the vital or generative power of nature, we shall, I think, best distinguish from the first, by calling it "growing." It is the mode of the farmer, the stock-raiser, the florist and the beekeeper.

And besides the first mode, which we have called "adapting," and the second mode, which we have called "growing," there is still a third mode in which, by men living in civilization, wealth is produced. In the first mode we make use of powers or qualities inherent in all material things; in the second we make use of powers or qualities inherent in all living things, vegetable or animal. But this third mode of production consists in the utilization of a power or tendency manifested only in man, and belonging to him by virtue of his peculiar gift of reason — that of exchanging or trading.

Yet not merely is it through exchange that the utilization in production of the highest powers both of the human factor and the natural factor become possible, but it seems to me that in itself exchange brings about a perceptible increase in the sum of wealth, and that even if we could ignore the matter in which it extends the power of the other two modes of production, this constitutes, in itself, a third mode of production.

Each of the two parties to an exchange aims to get, and as a rule does get, something that is more valuable to him than what he gives — that is to say, that represents to him a greater power of labor to satisfy desire. Thus there is in the transaction an actual increase in the sum of wealth, an actual production of wealth. A trading-vessel, for instance, penetrating to the Arctic, exchanges fish-hooks, harpoons, powder and guns, knives and mirrors, green spectacles and mosquito-nets for pelts. Each party to the exchange gets in return for what costs it comparatively little labor what would cost a great deal of labor to get by either of the other modes of production. Each gains by the act. Eliminating transportation, which belongs to the first mode of production, the joint wealth of both parties, the sum of the wealth of the world, is by the exchange itself increased.

This third mode of production let us call "exchanging." It is the mode of the merchant or trader, of the storekeeper; and of all the accessories, including in large measure transporters and their accessories.

We thus have as the three modes of production: 1) Adapting;

2) Growing; 3) Exchanging.

These modes seem to appear and to assume importance in the development of human society much in the order here given. They originate from the increase of the desires of men with increase of the means of satisfying them under pressure of the fundamental law of political economy, that men seek to satisfy their desires with the least exertion. In the primitive stage of human life the readiest way of satisfying desires is by adapting to human use what is found in existence. In a later and more settled stage it is discovered that certain desires can be more easily and more fully satisfied by utilizing the principle of growth and reproduction, as by cultivating vegetables and breeding animals. And in a still later period of development, it becomes obvious that certain desires can be better and more easily satisfied by exchange, which brings out the principle of cooperation more fully and powerfully than it could obtain among unexchanging economic units.

Chapter 3 — The Alleged Law of Diminishing Returns in Agriculture

Before proceeding to the subject of cooperation it is necessary to consider, if but to clear the way, what is treated in standard economic works since the time of Adam Smith as the most important law of production, and indeed of political economy as a whole. This is what is called "The Law of Diminishing Production," or more fully and exactly, "The Law of Diminishing Returns in Agriculture." Of it John Stuart Mill says:

> *This general law of agricultural industry is the most important proposition in political economy. Were the law different nearly all the phenomena of the production and distribution of wealth would be other than they are.*

This view of the importance of "the law of diminishing returns in agriculture" pervades the standard political economies, and is held by the most recent scholastic writers, such as Professor Walker of the United States and Professor Marshall of England, as by Mill and his predecessors. It arises from the relation of this alleged law to current apprehensions of the law of rent, and especially from the support which it seems to give the Malthusian doctrine that population tends to outrun subsistence — a support to which the long acceptance of that doctrine is due.

Thus, as the necessary consequence of this "law of diminishing returns in agriculture," John Stuart Mill says:

> *In all countries which have passed beyond a rather early stage in the progress of agriculture, every increase in the demand for food, occasioned by increased population, will always, unless there is a simultaneous improvement in production, diminish the share which on a fair division would fall to each individual...*

From this, results the important corollary, that the necessity of restraining population is not, as many persons believe, peculiar to a condition of great inequality of property. A greater number of people cannot, in any given state of civilization, be collectively so well provided for as a smaller. The niggardliness of nature, not the injustice of society, is the cause of the penalty attached to overpopulation. An unjust distribution of wealth does not even aggravate the evil, up but at most causes it to be somewhat earlier felt. It is in vain to say, that all mouths which the increase of mankind calls into existence bring with them hands. The new mouths require as much food as the old ones, and the hands do not produce as much.

As to the law itself, from which such tremendous consequences are constantly deduced — consequences which put us to the mental confusion of denying the justice of the Creator, and assuming that the Originating Spirit is so poor a contriver as to be constantly doing what any mere human host would be ashamed to be guilty of, bringing more guests to his table than could be fed — it is thus stated by Mill:

After a certain and not very advanced stage in the progress of agriculture; as soon, in fact, as mankind have applied to cultivation any energy, and have brought to it any tolerable tools; from that time it is the law of production from the land, that in any given state of agricultural skill and knowledge, by increasing the labor, the produce is not increased in equal degree; doubling labor does not increase the produce; or to express the same thing in other words, every increase of produce is obtained by a more than proportional increase in the application of labor to the land.

This law of diminishing returns in agriculture, it is further explained, applies also to mining, and in short to all the primary or extractive industries, which give the character of wealth to what was not before wealth, but not to those secondary or subsequent industries which add an additional increase of wealth. Thus since the law of diminishing productiveness in agriculture does not apply to the secondary industries, it is assumed that any increased application of labor (and capital) in manufacturing for instance, would continue to yield a proportionate and more than proportionate return. And as conclusive and axiomatic proof of this law of diminishing productiveness in agriculture, it is said that were it not for this peculiar law, the additional application of labor would result in a proportionately increased production from the same land, and one single farm would suffice to raise all the agricultural produce required to feed the whole population of the world, by mere increase in the application of labor.

This proposition seems to have been generally accepted by professional economists as a valid *reductio ad absurdum.* But analysis will show that this logical structure rests upon an unerring misapprehension; that there is in truth no special law of diminishing productiveness applying to agriculture, or to the extractive occupations. What has been misapprehended as a special law of diminishing returns in agriculture is in reality a general law, applying as well to manufacturing and exchanging, being in fact nothing less general than the spatial law of all material existence and movement — inorganic as well as organic.

This will appear if we consider the relation of space to production. But to do this thoroughly and at the same time to clear the way for considerations which may prove important in other parts of this work, I propose to begin by endeavoring to fix the meaning and nature of space and time

Chapter 4 — Space and Time

My purpose in this work is to explain the science of political economy so clearly that it may be understood by anyone of common ability who will give to it reasonable attention. I wish therefore to avoid, as far as possible, everything that savors of metaphysics.

Yet to trace to their root confusions involving current economic teachings and to clear the ground for a coherent political economy, it is necessary to fix the real meaning of two conceptions which belong to metaphysics, and which are beset by confusions that have not only disturbed the teaching of political economy, but of philosophy in the higher sense. These conceptions are those of space and time.

All material existence is in space and in time. Hence, the production of wealth, which in all its modes consists in the bringing about by human exertion of changes in the place or relation of material things, so as to fit them for the satisfaction of human desire, involves both space and time. This may seem like a truism — a fact so self-evident as not to need statement. But much disquisition has been wasted and much confusion caused by the failure of economists to keep this in mind. Hence, to start from firm foundations, we must see clearly what is really meant by space and time. Here we come into the very heart of metaphysics, at a point where the teachings of what passes for the highest philosophy are most perplexed and perplexing.

In asking ourselves what we really mean by space and time, we must have a care, for there is the danger that the habitual use of words as instruments of thought may lead to the error of treating what they express as objects of thought, or things, when they really express not things, but only qualities or relations of things. This is one of those sources of error in which Bacon in his figurative classification called Idols of the Forum. Though a word is a thing, in the sense that its verbal form may be made an object of thought, yet all words are not things in the sense of representing to the mind what apart from mere verbal form may be made an object of thought. To give a name to a form of words implying contradictions is to give name to what can be thought of only verbally, and which in any deeper sense than that is a negation — that is to say, nothing.

Yet this is the trick of much that today passes for the most profound philosophy, as it was the trick of Plato and of much that he put into the mouth of Socrates. To try it, make up a word signifying opposite qualities such as "lowhigh" or "squareround," or a phrase without thinkable meeting, such as a "fourth dimension of space." In this it will be wisest to use a tongue which, being foreign to the vernacular, is suggestive of learning. Latin, or Greek, has long been used for this purpose, but among English-speaking people German will now do as well if not better. Now, if you will persist for awhile in seeming to treat your new word or phrase as if you were really making it an object of deep thought, you will soon have others persuading themselves to think that they can also think of it, until finally, if it gets the scholastic vogue, the man frank enough to say that he can get no meaning from it will be put down as an ignorant fellow whose education has been neglected. This is really the same trick as standing on the street and gazing into the sky, as if you saw something unusual there, until a crowd gathers to look also, but it has made great reputations in philosophy.

Now, in truth, when we come to analyze our apprehensions of space and time, we see that they are conceptions, not of things in themselves existing, but of relations which things in themselves existing may hold to each other — space being a relation of extension or place between one thing and other things, such as far or near, hither or thither; and time being a relation of succession between one thing and other things, such as before or after, now and then. To think of space we must necessarily think of two points in space, and to make the relation of extension between them intelligible to our minds, we must also think of a third point which may serve as a measure of this relation. To think of time we must necessarily think of two points in appearance or disappearance, and to make this relation of sequence between them intelligible to our minds, we must also think of some third point which may serve as a measure of this relation.

Chapter 5 — The Relation of Space in Production

The laws of our physical being, to which I have already called attention, confine us within narrow limits to that part of the superficies of our sphere where the ocean of air enveloping it meets the solid surface. Physically we are air-breathing, or light-requiring land animals, who for our existence and all our production require place on the dry surface of our globe. And the fundamental perception of the concept of land is that of extension; that of affording standing-place or room.

But a fundamental perception is not always a first perception. Weight is a fundamental perception of air. But we realize this only by the exertion of reason, and long generations of men have lived, feeling the weight of air on every part of their bodies during every second of their lives, without ever realizing that air has weight. Perception is by contrast. What we always perceive neither attracts attention nor excites memory until brought into contrast with non-perception.

Even in the now short Atlantic trip the passenger becomes so accustomed to the constant throb of the engines as not to notice it, but is aroused by the silence when it stops. The visitor in a nail-mill is so deafened that speech seems impossible; but the men working there are said to talk to each other without difficulty and to find conversation hard when they get again into the comparative silence of the street.

Thus, while the fundamental quality of land is that of furnishing to men a place on which they may stand or move, this is not the quality first noticed. As settlers in a wooded country, where every foot of land must be cleared for use, come to regard trees as a nuisance to be got rid of, rather than as the source of value that in the progress of civilization they afterwards become, so in that rude stage of social development which we are accustomed to think of as the primary condition of mankind, where the mode of expending labor in production which most attracts attention is that we have called "adapting," land would be esteemed rich or poor according to its capacity of yielding to labor expended in this first mode, the fruits of the chase.

In the next higher stage of social development, in which that second mode of production, which we have called "growing," begins to assume most importance in social life, that quality of land which generally and strongly attracts attention is that which makes it useful in agriculture, and land would be esteemed rich or poor according to its capacity for yielding to labor expended in the breeding of animals and raising of crops.

But in a still higher stage of social development, attention begins to be largely given to the third mode of production, which we have called "exchanging," and land comes to be considered rich or poor according to its capacity of yielding to labor expended in trading. This is already the case in our great cities, where an enormous value attaches to land, not because of its capacity to provide wild animals to the hunter, nor yet because of its capacity to yield rich crops to the farmer, but because of its proximity to centers of exchange.

That the development of our modern economy began in what was still mainly the second stage of social development, when the use of land was usually regarded from the agricultural point of view, is, it seems to me, the explanation of an otherwise curious way of thinking about land that has pervaded economic literature since the time of the Physiocrats, and that still continues to pervade the scholastic political economy — a way of thinking that leads economic writers to treat land as though it were merely a place or substance on which vegetables and grain may be grown and cattle bred.

The followers of Quesnay saw that there is in the aggregate

production of wealth in civilization an unearned increment — an element which cannot be attributed to the earnings of labor or capital — and they gave to this increment of wealth, unearned so far as individuals are concerned, the name of net or surplus product. They rightly traced this unearned or surplus product to land, seeing that it constituted to the owners of land an income or return which remained to them after all expenditure of labor and investment of capital in production had been paid for. But they fell into error in assuming that what was indeed in their time and place the most striking and prominent use of land in production, that of agriculture, was its only use. And finding in agriculture the use of a power of nature essentially different from the power that is utilized in that first mode of production I have named "adapting," they jumped to the conclusion that the unearned increment of wealth sprang from the utilization of this principle. Hence they deemed agriculture the only productive occupation, and insisted that manufacture and commerce added nothing to the sum of wealth above what they took from it, and that the farmer was the only real producer.

This weakness in the thinking of the Physiocrats finally discredited their true and noble teachings, unpalatable as they necessarily were to the powerful interests who seemingly profit by social injustice. But the economists who succeeded Adam Smith, while they avoided the error into which the Physiocrats had fallen, avoided as well the great truth of which this had been an erroneous apprehension. Greedily accepting the excuse which the Malthusian theory offered for putting upon the laws of God responsibility for the misery and vice that flow from poverty, they fell into the habit of regarding land solely from the agricultural point of view, thus converting what is really the spatial law of all production into an alleged law of diminishing production in agriculture. Even Ricardo, who truly though very narrowly explained the law of rent, shows in all his arguments and illustrations an inability to free himself from thinking of land as relating only to agriculture, and of rent only as agricultural rent. And although in England the relative importance of agriculture has during all this century steadily and rapidly declined, the habit of thinking of land as a place or substance for agricultural operations is still kept up. Not merely is the law of diminishing production in agriculture still taught as a special law of nature in the latest works treated as authoritative in colleges and universities, but in speaking of land and of rent most English writers will be found to have really in mind agricultural land or agricultural rent.

What is true of England is true of the United States except so far as the influence of the single tax has been felt. But the greatest difficulty which the single tax propaganda meets in the United States is the widespread idea, sedulously fostered by those who should know better, that nonagricultural workers have no interest in the land question and that concentrating taxes on land values means increasing the taxes of farmers. To fostering this fallacy all the efforts of the credited organs of education are directed.

The relation of space to all production may be readily seen. The concentration of labor in space tends up to a certain point to increase the productiveness of labor; but increase of production with increased application of labor to any given area cannot go on indefinitely. A point is reached at which the further application of labor in the given area, though it may for a time result in greater aggregate production, yields a less proportionate production, and finally a point is reached where the further application of labor ceases even to increase the aggregate result.

This law is not peculiar to agriculture nor to the second mode of production which I have called "growing." The exertion of human labor in the production of wealth requires a space; not merely standing or resting space, but moving space — space for the movements of the human body and its organs, space for the storage and changing in place of materials and tools and products. This is as true of the tailor, the carpenter, the machinist, the merchant or the clerk, as of the farmer or stock-grower, or of the fisherman or miner. One occupation may require more elbow-room or tool-room or storage-room than another, but they all alike require space, and so must come to a point where any gain from concentrating labor in space ceases, and further concentration results in a proportionate lessening of product, and finally in an absolute decline. The same law, first of increasing, then of diminishing returns, from the concentration of labor in space, which the exponents of the doctrine of diminishing returns in agriculture say is peculiar to that occupation, is nothing more or less than the spatial law of material existence.

We have only to think of it to see that what is called the law of diminishing returns in agriculture applies to the making of bricks as fully as to the growing of beets. A single man engaged in making a thousand bricks would greatly waste labor if he were to diffuse his exertions over a square mile, digging and burning the clay for one brick here and for another some distance apart. His exertion would yield a much larger return if more closely concentrated in space. But there is a point in this concentration in space where the increase of exertion will begin to diminish its proportionate yield. In the same superficial area required for the production of one brick, two bricks may be produced to advantage. But this concentration of labor in space cannot be continued indefinitely without diminishing the return and finally bringing production to a stop. To get the clay for a thousand bricks without use of more surface of the Earth than is required to get the clay for one brick would involve, even if it were possible at all, an enormous loss in the productiveness of the labor. And so if an attempt were made to put a thousand men to work in making bricks on an area in which two men might work with advantage, the result would be not merely that the exertion of the thousand men could not produce five hundred times as much as the exertion of two men, but that it would produce nothing at all. Men so crowded would prevent each other from working.

Or let us take that part of the production of bricks that of all parts requires least space — that which consists merely in the storage of bricks after they are made. Though two bricks may be rested on top of one another without any more use of superficial area than is required for the resting of one brick, this is not true of a thousand bricks, nor even of a hundred. Much less than one hundred bricks so placed would become so unstable as to fall with the slightest jar or breeze. Before ten bricks had been rested one on top of another it would become evident that any further extension of the perpendicular would require an extension of the base. And even with such extension of base as would permit of perpendicular stability, a point would finally be reached where, even if the surface continued solid, the weight of the upper bricks would crush the lower bricks to powder. Thus it is no more possible indefinitely to store bricks on a given area than on a given area indefinitely to grow beets.

Up to a point, moreover, which is about waist-high for an ordinary man, it requires less exertion to place or take from place the last brick than the first brick, or in other words, labor at this point is more productive. But once this point of greatest productiveness is reached, the productiveness of labor begins to decline with the further application of labor on the same area, until the point of no return or non-productiveness is reached. The region of this point of no return to the further application of labor in the storing of bricks on a given area may be delayed by such labor-saving devices as the wheelbarrow and steam engine, but it cannot be prevented.

There is a point in the application of labor to the storage of bricks on any given area, whether a square foot or square mile, where the application of successive "doses of labor" must cease to yield proportionate returns, and finally where they must cease to yield any return.

Thus the law of diminishing returns, which has been held as peculiar to agriculture, is as fully shown in the mere storage of bricks as it is in the growing of crops or the breeding of animals. The point of greatest efficiency or maximum productiveness in the application of labor to land exists in all modes and all forms of production. It results in fact from nothing more nor less than the universal law or condition that all material existence, and consequently all production of wealth, requires space.

Chapter 6 — The Relation of Time in Production

As space is the relation of things in extension, so time is a relation of things in sequence. All production of wealth takes place in sequence and requires time. The tree must be felled before it can be hewn or sawed into lumber; lumber must be seasoned before it can be used in building or wrought into the manifold articles made of wood. Ore must be taken from the vein before it can be smelted into iron, or from that form turned into steel or any of the manifold articles made from iron or steel. Seeds must be planted before they can germinate; there must be a considerable interval of time before the young shoots can show themselves above the ground; then a longer interval before they can grow and ripen and produce after their order; the grain must be harvested and ground before it can be converted into meal or flour. In exchanging, time is required even for the concurrence and expression of human wills which result in the agreement to exchange, and still more for the actual transference of things which completes the exchange. In short, time is a necessary element or condition in all exertion of labor in production.

Now, from this necessary element or condition of all production, time, there result consequences similar to those which result from the other necessary element or condition of all production, space. That is to say, there is a law governing and limiting the concentration of labor in time, as there is a law governing and limiting the concentration of labor in space. Thus there is in all forms of production a point at which the concentration of labor in time gives the largest proportionate result; after which the further concentration of labor in time tends to a diminution of proportionate result, and finally to prevent results.

Thus there is a certain degree of concentration of labor in time (the intensity of exertion), by which the individual can in any productive occupation accomplish on the whole the largest result. But if a man work harder than this, endeavoring to concentrate more exertion in a shorter time, it will be to the relative and finally to the absolute loss of productiveness — a principle which gives its point to the fable of the hare and the tortoise.

And so, if I go to a builder and say to him, "In what time and at what price will you build me such and such a house?" he would, after thinking, name a time, and a price based on it. This specification of time would be essential, and would involve a certain concentration of labor in time as the point of largest return or least cost. This I would soon find if, not quarreling with the price, I ask him largely to lessen the time. If I were a man to whom cost is nothing and time everything, I might get the builder somewhat to reduce the time in which he would agree, under bond, to build a house; but only by greatly increasing the price, until finally a point would be reached where he would not consent to build the house in less time no matter what the price.

And so, although the concentration of labor in agriculture may with decreasing efficiency hasten beyond the normal point the majority of vegetables or fruit or even of animals, yet the point of absolute non-productiveness of further applications of labor is soon reached, and no amount of human exertion applied in any way we have yet discovered could bring wheat from the seed to the ear, or the chick from the egg to the laying hen, in a week.

The importance in political economy of this principle that all production of wealth requires time as well as labor we shall see later on; but the principle that time is a necessary element in all production we must take into account from the very first.

Chapter 7 — Co-operation: Its Two Ways

Co-operation means joint action; the union of efforts to a common end.

All increase in the productive power of man over that with which nature endows the individual comes from the co-operation of individuals. But there are two ways in which this co-operation may take place:

1) By the combination of effort. In this way, individuals may accomplish what exceeds the full power of the individual.

2) By the separation of effort. In this way, the individual may accomplish for more than one what does not require the full power of the individual.

To illustrate: the first way of co-operation, the combination of labor, enables a number of men to remove a rock or to raise a log that would be too heavy for them separately. In this way men can join themselves, as it were, into one stronger man.

Examples of the same principle in a more elaborate state of society are to be found in the formation of joint-stock companies — the union of many small capitals to accomplish works such as the building of railroads, the construction of steamships, the direction of factories, etc., which require greater capitals than are possessed by one man.

But while great advantages result from the ability of individuals, by the combination of labor, to concentrate themselves as it were into one larger man, there are other times in which an individual could accomplish more if he could divide himself, as it were, into a number of smaller men.

Thus in sailing a boat, one man of extraordinary strength would be equal to two men of half his strength only in such exertions as rowing, hoisting the heavier sails, or the like. In other things, two men of ordinary strength would be able to do far more than one man of double strength, since where he would have to stop one thing to do another, they could do both things at once. Thus while he would have to anchor in order to rest, they could move on without stopping, one sailing the boat while the other slept.

How often now when beset by calls or duties which require not so much strength as time, does a thought occur, "I wish I could divide myself into half a dozen." What the division of labor does is to permit men, as it were, so to divide themselves, thus enormously increasing their total effectiveness.

To illustrate from the example used before: while at times Tom, Dick, Harry and Jim might each wish to move logs, at other times they might each need to get something from the village two days' journey distant. To satisfy this need individually would thus require two days' effort on the part of each. But if Tom goes alone, performing the errands for all, and the others each do half a day's work for him, the result is that all get at the expense of half a day's effort what would otherwise have required two days' effort.

It is in this manner that labor is saved by the second way of cooperation, the separation of effort, or to continue the term adopted by Adam Smith, the division of labor. It permits the accomplishment of equal results with less exertion, or larger results with equal exertion. But out of this primary saving of exertion arise other savings of exertion.

Take for instance the baking of bread. To bake a loaf of bread requires the application of a certain amount of heat for a certain time to a certain amount of dough. To heat an oven to this point requires a certain expenditure of fuel; to maintain it for this time a certain other expenditure of fuel; and a certain expenditure of fuel is lost in the cooling of the oven after the bread is baked. To bake one loaf of bread in an ordinary oven thus requires a much greater relative expenditure of fuel than is required to bake as many loaves as the oven will hold; and the larger oven will bake more loaves with a proportionately less expenditure of fuel than a smaller one, since the loss of heat that escapes from the work of baking is relatively less; and if one batch of bread is succeeded by another batch without suffering the oven to cool, another relative saving is made. The concentration of the work of baking bread effects a great saving of labor in the item of fuel allowed. And it is so with other items.

The saving thus made in the concentration of work arises not only from physical laws but from mental laws as well. All our doing or accomplishing of things, except those that may be referred to instinct, require in the first place the exertion of conscious thought. We see this in the child as it learns to walk, to talk, to read and to write. We see this as adults when we begin to do things new to us, as to speak a foreign tongue, to write shorthand, or to use a typewriter or a bicycle. But as we do the same things again and again, the mental exertion becomes less and less, until we come to do them automatically and without consciously thinking of how we do them.

Now the result of what regarded from the standpoint of the whole or industrial organism is the division of labor in the production of wealth, is that the individual does fewer things but does them oftener. It is thus from the standpoint of the individual the concentration of effort or of labor, and so from the standpoint of the things to be done it involves a similar concentration in place and time.

Thus, when instead of each individual or each family endeavoring to hunt, fish, and obtain vegetables, build habitations and make clothing or tools, for the satisfaction of their own needs, some devote themselves to doing one thing and some to doing another of the things required for the satisfaction of general needs, what is the separation of function from the standpoint of the all or industrial whole is a concentration of function in its units, and special trades and vocations are developed. And as the social organism grows by increase in numbers or the widening of the circle of exchanges, or both, this differentiation of function between its units tends constantly to increase, augmenting the efficiency of the productive powers of man to a degree to which we can assign no limits, and of which the marvelous increase in productive power which so strikingly characterizes our modern civilization affords but a faint forecast.

In civilized society where the division of labor has been carried to great lengths, we are so used to it that is hard to realize how much we owe to it, and how utterly different our life would be without it. But as one tries to think to what we should be reduced without division of labor, he will see how large a part it plays in the production of wealth — so large, indeed, that without it man as we know him could not exist. Take for instance the providing of clothing. If each one had to make his own clothing from the raw material, he could get nothing better than leaves or skins. Even with all the advantages which the division of labor gives in the making of cloth, of needles, thread, buttons, etc., let anyone unused to it set himself to the making of a garment. He will soon realize how hard it is to make the first one; how much easier and better the second is made than the first, the third than the second, and so on, until the process ceases to require thought and becomes automatic. When by means of the division of labor, the making of clothing is so far concentrated that the clothing for some dozens or scores of men can be made together, then individuals can devote themselves solely to the making of clothes, with greatly increased economy. As a concentration of clothes-making proceeds further, and the making of clothes for hundreds, thousands, tens of thousands, and even hundreds of thousands of individuals is by the development of the ready-made clothing industry brought together, greater and greater economies become possible. Separate individuals devote themselves to the making of particular garments, and then to the making of particular parts or to particular processes. Instead of one tailor cutting out a garment with a pair of shears and then proceeding to make it in all its parts, others who do nothing else cut out scores of garments at once with great knives; the operations of basting, lining, buttonholing, etc., are performed by different people who devote themselves to doing these things alone, and this work is aided by powerful machines, the use of which becomes possible with the larger scale and greater continuity of employment this concentration permits.

This concentration and specialization of work brings about the development of labor-saving machinery of all kinds. The essential quality of the machine is its adaptation for the doing of certain special things. The human body considered as a machine is of all machines that which is best adapted for the doing of the greatest variety of things. But for doing only one thing, for the increase of quantity at the expense of variety, man is able to make machines which within a narrow range are far superior to the tools nature gives him. And the same principle governs the employment of forces other than the force he can command in his muscles. The utilization of winds and tides and currents and falling streams, of steam and of electricity, and chemical attractions and repulsions, is dependent on this concentration.

Thus the division of labor involves and proceeds from the concentration of effort for the satisfaction of desires. It begins when there are two individuals who cooperate; it increases and becomes productive of greater and greater economies with the increase of the number who thus cooperate.

We may perhaps best analyze the advantages that result from

the cooperation of labor as follows:

A. The combination of labor permits a number of individuals by direct union of their powers to accomplish what severally would be impossible.

B. The division of labor, with the concentration and cooperation it involves, permits the doing for many (or a larger number) of what may with a less expenditure be done by one (or by a smaller number):

1. By the saving up of time and effort, as in the preceding illustration, where one man goes on a journey which to accomplish severally four men would have to make.

2. By utilizing the differing powers of individuals, as where those who excel in certain qualities do the things for which such qualities are best adapted, thus practically bringing up the level of the accomplishment of all to that of the highest qualities of each.

3. By increasing skill, consequent upon those who do a larger amount of that same kind of work being able to acquire facility in it.

4. By accumulating knowledge.

5. By utilizing the advantages of doing things on a large scale instead of on a small scale, and of doing them successively instead of separately.

6. By utilizing the natural forces, and by the invention and use of machines and of improved processes, for the use of which the large-scale production gives advantages.

Chapter 8 — Cooperation: Its Two Kinds

We have seen that there are two ways or modes in which co-operation increases productive power. If we ask how cooperation is itself brought about, we see that there is in this also a distinction, and that cooperation is of essentially two different kinds. The line of distinction as to what I have called the *ways* of cooperation, and have in the last chapter considered, is as to the method of action or how of accomplishment; the line of distinction as to what I shall call the *kinds* of cooperation, and am about in this chapter to consider, is as to the method of union or how of initiative.

There is one kind of cooperation, proceeding as it were from without, which results from the conscious direction of a controlling will to a definite end. This we may call directed or conscious co-operation. There is another kind of cooperation, proceeding as it were from within, which results from a correlation in the actions of independent wills, each seeking but its own immediate purpose, and careless, if not indeed ignorant, of the general result. This we may call spontaneous or unconscious cooperation.

The movement of a great army is a good type of directed cooperation. Here the actions of many individuals are subordinated to and directed by one conscious will, becoming, as it were, its body and executing its thought. The providing of a great city with all the manifold things which are constantly needed by its inhabitants is a good type of spontaneous cooperation. This kind of cooperation is far wider, far finer, far more strongly and delicately organized, than the kind of cooperation involved in the movements of an army, yet it is brought about not by subordination to the direction of one conscious will, which knows the general result at which it aims; but by the correlation of actions originating in many independent wills, each aiming at its own small purpose without thought of the general result.

The one kind of cooperation seems to have its analogue in those related movements of our body which we are able consciously to direct. The other kind of cooperation seems to have its analogue in the correlation of the innumerable movements, of which we are unconscious, that maintain the bodily frame — motions which in their complexity, delicacy and precision far transcend our powers of conscious direction, yet by whose perfect adjustment to each other and to the purpose of the whole keep the human body in life and vigor.

Much of the cooperation of man in producing social effects is of the nature of that by which a ship is sailed. It involves the delegation to individuals of the power of arranging and directing what others shall do, thus securing for the general action the advantages of one managing and correlating intelligence. But while cooperation of this kind is indispensable to producing certain results by conjoint action, it is helpless or all but helpless to bring about certain other results involving a longer series and more complicated and delicate actions and adjustments.

To illustrate: a bird structurally is a machine as a ship is a machine, which the conscious will of the bird, controlling certain voluntary movements, causes to rise or fall, to sweep in this direction or in that, to be carried at the gale or to tack in its teeth, in short to execute all the movements of which this bird machine is capable. But the conscious will that controls the voluntary motions of the bird, the intelligence that is the captain of this aerial craft, will not account for the machine itself; for its consummate arrangements and adjustments and adaptations. These transcend not only the intelligence of the bird, but also the highest human intelligence. The union of lightness with strength, of rigidity with flexibility, of grace with power; the appropriateness of material, the connection and relation of parts, the economies of space and energy and function, the applications of what are to us the most complex and recondite of physical laws, make the bird, as a machine, far superior to the best and highest machines of man's construction.

Savages must at times ponder over the mystery of the egg — for to them as to us it would be an insoluble mystery. But it is the ship, not the bird, that would most excite their wonder and admiration, for the savage would see in the ship as soon as he came close to it, not a thing that grew, but a thing that was made — a higher expression of the same power which he himself exercises in his own rude constructions. He would see in it, when he came to look closely, but a vastly greater and better canoe. Since a larger canoe than one man can build may be built by the same man if he can unite the exertions of others in cutting, rolling, hewing and hollowing a great log, so it would seem to our savage that it was in this way that the ship of civilization was built. And the admiration which the ship would excite in him would be an admiration of the men who sailed it, whom he naturally would take to be the men who built it, or at least the men who could build it. The superiority of the ship to the rude canoes with which he was familiar he would attribute to superiority of their personal qualities — their greater knowledge and skill and power. They would indeed seem to him at first as very gods.

Yet the savage would be wrong. The superiority of the ship does not indicate the superiority of individual men. If driven ashore with the loss of their ship and all its contents, these men would be more helpless than so many of his own people, and would find it more difficult to make even a canoe. Even if they had saved tools and stores, it would only be after long toil that they could succeed in building some rude, small craft unfitted for long voyage and rough weather, and not in any respect comparable with their ship. For a modern ship is more akin to a growth than a direct construction — in that as between the kind of cooperation required for its production and that which suffices for that of a canoe, there is a difference which suggests something not altogether unlike the difference between a work of nature and a work of man.

The cooperation required in the making of a large canoe or in the sailing of a ship is exceedingly simple as compared to that involved in the construction and equipment of a well-found, first-class ship. The actual putting together, according to the plans of the naval architect, of the separate parts and materials which compose such a ship, would require, after they had been assembled, some directed cooperation. But if cooperation of this kind could suffice for even putting the parts together after they had been made and assembled, how could it suffice for making those various parts from the forms in which nature offers their material, and assembling them in the place where they were to be put together?

Consider the timbers, the planks, the spars; the iron and steel of various kinds and forms; the copper, the brass, the bolts, screws, spikes, chains; the ropes, of steel and hemp and cotton; the canvas of various textures; the blocks and winches and windlasses; the pumps, the boats, the sextants, the chronometers, the spy-glasses and patent logs, the barometers and thermometers, charts, nautical almanacs, rockets and colored lights; food, clothing, tools, medicines and furniture, and all the various things, which it would be tiresome fully to specify, that go into the construction and furnishing of a first-class sailing ship of modern type. Directed cooperation never did, and I do not think in the nature of things ever could, make and assemble such a variety of products, involving as many of them do the use of costly machinery and consummate skill, and the existence of subsidiary products and processes.

When the shipbuilder receives an order for such a ship as this he does not send men out into the forest, he does not direct some to mine iron ore, and others copper ore, and others lead ore, and others still to dig the coal with which these ores are to be smelted, and the fire-clay for this melting-vessel; some to plant hemp, and some to plant cotton, and others to breed silkworms; some to make glass, others to kill beasts for their hides and tallow, some to get pitch and rosin, oil, paint, paper, felt and mercury. Nor does he attempt to direct to the manifold operations by which these raw materials are to be brought into the required forms and combinations, and assembled in the place where the ship is to be built. Such a task would transcend the wisdom and power of a Solomon. What he does is to avail himself of the resources of a high civilization, for without that he would be helpless, and to make use for his purposes of the unconscious cooperation by which, without any general direction, the efforts of many men, working in many different places and in occupations which cover almost the whole field of minutely diversified industry, each animated solely by the effort to obtain the satisfaction of his personal desires in what to him is the easiest way, have brought together the materials and productions needed for the putting together of such a ship.

A modern ship, like a modern railway, is a product of modern civilization; of that correlation of individual efforts in which what we call civilization essentially consists; of that unconscious co-operation which does not come by personal direction, as it were from without, but grows, as it were from within, by the relation of the efforts of individuals, each seeking the satisfaction of individual desires. A mere master of men, though he might command the services of billions, could not make such a ship unless in a civilization prepared for it. A Pharaoh that built pyramids, a Ghengis Khan who raised mounds of skulls, an Alexander, a Caesar, or even a Henry VIII could not do it.

The kind of cooperation which I have illustrated by the tacking of a ship is a very simple matter. It could be readily taught. But that kind of cooperation which is involved in the making of such a ship is a much deeper and more complex matter. It is beyond the power of conscious direction to order or bring about. It can no more be advanced or improved by any exertion of the power of directing the conscious actions of men than the conscious will of the individual can add a cubit to his stature. The only thing that conscious direction can do to aid it is to let it alone; to give it freedom to grow, leaving men free to seek the gratification of their own desires in the ways that to them seem best. To attempt to apply that kind of cooperation which requires direction from without to the work proper for that kind of cooperation which requires direction from within, is like asking the carpenter who can build a chicken-house to build a chicken also.

This is the fatal defect of all forms of socialism — the reason of the fact, which all observation shows, that any attempt to carry conscious regulation and direction beyond the narrow sphere of social life in which it is necessary, inevitably works injury, hindering even what it is intended to help.

It is only in independent action that the full powers of man may be utilized. The subordination of one human will to another human will, while it may in certain ways secure unity of action, must always where intelligence is needed, involve loss of productive power. This we see exemplified in slavery and where governments have undertaken (as is the tendency of all government) unduly to limit the freedom of the individual. But where unity of effort, or rather combination of effort, can be secured while leaving full freedom to the individual, the whole of productive power may still be utilized and the result be immeasurably greater.

Imagine such an aggregation of men in which it was attempted to secure, by the external direction involved in socialistic theories, that division of labor which grows up naturally in society where men are left free. For the intelligent direction thus required an individual man or individual men must be selected, for even if there be angels and archangels in the world that is invisible to us, they are not at our command.

Taking no note of the difficulties which universal experience shows always to attend the choice of the depositaries of power, and ignoring the inevitable tendency to tyranny and oppression — even if the very wisest and best of men were selected for such purposes — simply consider the task that would be put upon them in the ordering and supervision of the almost infinitely complex and constantly changing relations involved in a civilized community. The task transcends the power of human intelligence at its very highest. It is evidently as much beyond the ability of conscious direction as is the correlation of the processes that maintain the human body in health and vigor.

This mind of ours, this conscious intelligence that perceives, compares, judges and wills, wondrous and far-reaching as are its powers, is like the eye that may look to far-off suns and milky ways, but cannot see its own mechanism. This body of ours in which our mind is encased, this infinitely complex and delicate machine through which we become conscious of the external world, exists only by virtue of unconscious intelligence which works while conscious intelligence rests; which is on guard while it sleeps; which wills without its concurrence and plans without its contriving, of which it has almost no direct knowledge and over which it has almost no direct control.

And so it is with the spontaneous, unconscious cooperation of individuals which, going on in the industrial body, conjoins individual efforts in the production of wealth, to the enormous increase in productive power, and distributes the product among the units of which it is composed. To ascertain the nature and laws of such cooperation is the primary province of political economy.

Chapter 9 — The Office of Exchange in Production

The act of exchange is that of deliberately parting with one thing for the purpose and as a means of getting another thing. It is an act that involves foresight, calculation, judgment — qualities in which reason differs from instinct.

All living things that we know of cooperate in some kind and to some degree. So far as we can see, nothing that lives can live in and for itself alone. But man is the only one who cooperates by exchanging, and he may be distinguished from all the numberless species that with him tenant the earth as the exchanging animal. Of them all he is the only one who seeks to obtain one thing by giving another. No other animal uses bait to attract its prey; no other animal plants edible seeds that it may gather the produce. No other animal gives another what it would like to have in order to receive in return what it likes better. But such acts come naturally to man with his maturity, and are of his distinguishing principle.

Exchange is the great agency by which what I have called the spontaneous or unconscious cooperation of man in the production of wealth is brought about, and economic units are welded into that social organism which is the Greater Leviathan.

Of the three modes of production which I have distinguished as adapting, growing and exchanging, the last is that by which alone the higher applications of the modes of adapting and growing are made available. Were it not for exchange the cooperation of individuals in the production of wealth could go no further than it might be carried by the natural instincts that operate in the formation of the family, or by that kind of cooperation in which individual wills are made subordinate to another individual will. These, it is evident, would not suffice for the lowest stage of civilization. For not only does slavery itself, which requires that the slaves shall be fed and clothed, involve some sort of exchange, though a very inadequate one, but the labor of slaves must be supplemented by exchange to permit the slave-owner to enjoy any more than the rudest satisfactions.

Many if not most of the writers on political economy have treated exchange as a part of distribution. On the contrary, it properly belongs to production. It is by exchange and through exchange that man obtains and is able to exert the power of cooperation which with the advance of civilization so enormously increases his ability to produce wealth.

The motive of exchange is the primary postulate of political economy, the universal fact that men seek to gratify their desires with the least exertion. This leads men by a universal impulse to seek to gratify their desires by exchange wherever they can thus obtain the gratification of desire with less exertion than any other way; and this is from the very origin of human society, and increasingly with its advance, the easiest way of procuring the satisfaction of the greatest number of desires.

And in addition to the laws already explained, there is another law or condition of nature related to man which is taken advantage of to the enormous increase of productive power in exchange: the office of competition in production.

That "competition is the life of trade," is an old and true adage. But in current thought and current literature there is so much assumption that competition is an evil that it is worthwhile to examine its cause and office in the production of wealth. Much of this assumption that competition is an evil that should be restricted in the higher interests of society springs from the desire of men unduly to profit at the expense of their fellows by distorting natural laws of the distribution of wealth. This is true of the form of socialism which was known in the time of Adam Smith as the mercantile system or theory, and which still exists under the general name of protectionism. Much of it again has a nobler origin, coming from a righteous indignation with the monstrous inequalities in the existing distribution of wealth throughout the civilized world, coupled with a mistaken assumption that these inequalities are due to competition.

I do not propose here to treat either of protectionism or socialism proper, my purpose being not that of controversy or refutation, but merely that of discovering and explaining the natural laws with which a science of political economy is concerned.

The competition of men with their fellows in the production of wealth has its origin in the impulse to satisfy desires with the least expenditure of exertion. Competition is indeed the life of trade, in a deeper sense than that it is a mere facilitator of trade. It is the life of trade in the sense that its spirit or impulse is identical to the spirit or impulse of trade. Competition brings trade, and consequently service, to its just level, and is therefore necessary to civilization.

*They who, seeing how men are forced by competition to the extreme of human wretchedness, jump to the conclusion that competition should be abolished, are like those who, seeing a house burn down, would prohibit the use of fire.

The air we breathe exerts upon every square inch of our bodies a pressure of fifteen pounds. Were this pressure exerted only on one side, it would pin us to the ground and crush us to a jelly. But being exerted on all sides, we move under it with perfect freedom. It not only does not inconvenience us, but it serves such indispensable purposes that, relieved of its pressure, we should die.

So it is with competition. Where there exists a class denied all right to the element necessary to life and labor, competition is one-sided, and as population increases must press the lowest class into virtual slavery, and even starvation. But where the natural rights of all are secured, then competition, acting on every hand — between employers as between employed; between buyers as between sellers — can injure no one. On the contrary it becomes the most simple, most extensive, most elastic, and most refined system of cooperation, that, in the present stage of social development, and in the domain where it will freely act, we can rely on for the coordination of industry and the economizing of social forces.

In short, competition plays just such a part in the social organism as those vital impulses which are beneath consciousness do in the bodily organism. With it, as with them, it is only necessary that it should be free.

---

* *These last four paragraphs are taken from George's* Protection or Free Trade *(1886), Chapter 28. In the original edition of* The Science of Political Economy, *the very short and clearly unfinished chapter titled "Office of Competition in Production" was followed by the pencilled note, "Leave six pages." — L. D.*

Chapter 10 — Order of the Three Factors of Production

All economists give the factors of production as three: land, labor and capital. And without exception that I know of, they maintain them in this order. This, indeed, is the natural order; the order of their appearance. The world, so far as political economy takes cognizance of it, began with land. Reason tells us that land, with all its powers and potentialities, including even all vegetable and animal life, existed before man was. But whether still "formless and void," or already instinct with the lower forms of life, so long as there was in the world only the economic element land, production in the economic sense could not be, and there was no wealth. When man appeared, and the economic element labor was united to the economic element land, production began, and its product, wealth, resulted. At length (for in the myths and poems in which mankind have expressed all the wisest could tell of our far beginnings, they have always loved to picture a golden age devoid of care), the greater power that could be gained by using wealth in aid of labor was seen, and a third factor of production, capital, appeared.

But between this third factor and the two factors which preceded it, a difference in nature and importance is to be noted. Land and labor are original and necessary factors. They cannot be resolved into each other, and they are indispensable to production, being necessary to production in all its modes. But capital is not an original factor. It is a compound or derivative factor, resulting from the union of the two original factors, land and labor. It is not indispensable to production, being necessary, as before explained, not in all modes of production, but only in some modes. Nevertheless, the part that it bears in production is so separable, and the convenience that is served by distinguishing it from the original factors is so great, that it has been properly recognized by the earliest and by all subsequent writers in political economy as a separate factor; and the three elements by whose union wealth is produced in the civilized state are given by the names and in the order of 1) land, 2) labor, and 3) capital.

It may seem to the reader superfluous that I should lay such stress upon the order of the three factors of production, for it is not more self-evident that the mother must precede the child than that land must precede labor, and that labor must precede capital. But I dwell upon this question of order because it is the key to confusions which have brought the teaching of the science of political economy to absurdity and stultification. Indeed, those writers who have condescended to define their terms have recognized, in these definitions, the natural order of the three factors of production. But whoever will follow them will see that without seeming conscious of it themselves they soon slip into a reversal of this order, and, literally making the last first, proceed to assume that capital is the prime factor in production. Socialism, which gives such undue prominence to capital and yet is so completely at sea as to the real nature and functions of capital, has the root of its absurdities in the teachings of the scholastic economists.

But the results of this confusion as to the nature and order of the factors of production will be more fully treated when we come to consider the distribution of wealth. All that it is necessary to do here is to point out the true order of the factors of production and to make clear what they are. Let us proceed to consider them one by one.

Land

Man produces by drawing from nature. Land, in political economy, is the term for that from which he draws — for that which must exist before he himself can exist. In other words, the term land in political economy means the natural or passive element in production, and includes the whole external world accessible to man, with all its powers and qualities, except those portions of it which are for a time included in man's body or in his products, and which therefore temporarily belong to the categories of man and wealth, passing again in their re-absorption by nature into the category of land.

The original and ordinary meaning of the word, land, is that of dry superficies all the earth as distinguished from water or air. But man, as distinguished from the denizens of the water or the air, is primarily a land animal. The dry surface of the earth is his habitat, from which alone he can venture upon or make use of any other element, or obtain access to any other material thing or potency. Thus, as a law term, land means not merely the dry superficies of the earth, but all that is above and all that may be below it, from zenith to nadir. For the same reasons the word land receives like extension of meaning when used as a term of political economy, and comprises all having material form that man has received or can receive from nature, that is to say, from God.

Thus the term "land" in political economy means the natural or passive factor, on which and by or through which labor produces, and can alone produce.

But that land is only a passive factor in production must be carefully kept in mind. It is a thing, not a person, and though the tendency to personification leads not merely in poetry but in common speech to the use of phrases which attribute sentiment and action to land, it is important to remember that when we speak of a smiling, a sullen, or an angry landscape, or of the Earth giving or the Earth receiving, or of nature tempting or forbidding, we are merely using figures of speech more forcibly or more gracefully to express our own feelings by reflection from inanimate objects. In the production of wealth land cannot act; it can only be acted upon.

Nor is this principle changed or avoided when we use the word land as expressive of the people who own land. Landowners, as landowners, take no part in production whatever. Land cannot know whether men regard it as property or not, nor does that fact in any degree affect its powers. Sand is sand and gold is gold, and the rain falls and the sun shines, as little affected by the moral considerations that men recognize as the telegraph-wire is affected by the meaning of the messages that pass through it, or as the rock is affected by the twitter of the birds that fly over it.

I speak of this because although their definition of land as a factor in production is precisely that which I have given, there is to be found in the accepted treatises on political economy a constant tendency to the assumption that landowners, through their ownership of land, contribute to production.

That the persons whom we call landowners may contribute their labor or their capital to production is of course true, but that they should contribute to production as landowners, by virtue of that ownership, is as ridiculously impossible as that the belief of a lunatic in his ownership of the moon should be the cause of her brilliancy.

Labor

All human actions, or at least all conscious human actions, have their source in desire and their end and aim in the satisfaction of desire. Exertion is the intermediary action by which desire secures its aim in satisfaction. The economic term for this exertion is labor. It is the active, and from the human standpoint, the primary or initiative, factor in all production — that which being applied to land brings about all the changes conducive to the satisfaction of desire that it is possible for man to make in the material world.

In political economy there is no other term for this exertion than labor. That is to say, the term labor includes all human exertion in the production of wealth, whatever its mode. In common parlance we often speak of brain labor and hand labor as though they were entirely distinct kinds of exertion, and labor is often spoken of as though it involved only muscular exertion. But in reality any form of labor, that is to say, any form of human exertion in the production of wealth requires the human brain as truly as the human hand, and would be impossible without the exercise of mental faculties on the part of the laborer.

As land is the natural or passive factor in all production, so labor is the human or active factor. As such, it is the initiatory factor. All production results from the action of labor on land, and hence it is truly said that labor is the producer of all wealth.

Capital

The primary factors of production are labor and land, and from their union all production comes. Their concrete product is wealth, which is land modified by labor so as to fit or better fit it for the satisfaction of human desires. What is usually distinguished as the third factor of production, capital, is, as we have seen, a form or use of wealth.

Capital, which is not in itself a distinguishable element, but which, it must always be kept in mind, consists of wealth applied to the aid of labor in further production, is not a primary factor. There can be production without it, and there must have been production without it, or it could not in the first place have appeared. It is a secondary and compound factor, coming after and resulting from the union of labor and land in the production of wealth. It is in essence labor raised by a second union with land to a third or higher power. But it is to civilized life so necessary and important as to be rightfully accorded in political economy the place of a third factor in production. Without the use of capital man could raise himself but little above the level of the animals.

It is to be observed that capital of itself can do nothing. It is always a subsidiary, never an initiatory factor. The initiatory factor is always labor. That is to say, in the production of wealth labor always uses capital, is never used by capital. This is not merely literally true, when by the term capital we mean the thing capital, it is also true when we personify the term and mean by it not the thing capital, but the owners of capital. The capitalist pure and simple, the man who merely controls capital, has in his hands the power of assisting labor to produce. But purely as capitalist he cannot exercise that power. It can be exercised only by labor. To utilize it he must himself exercise at least some of the functions of labor, or he must put his capital, on some terms, at the use of those who do.

I speak of this because it is the habit, not only of common speech but of many writers on political economy, to speak as though capital were the initiatory factor in production, and as if capital or capitalists employed labor; whereas in fact, no matter what the form of the arrangement for the use of capital, it is always labor that starts production and is aided by capital; never capital that starts production and is aided by labor.

It cannot be too clearly kept in mind that labor is the only producer either of wealth or of capital. Appropriation can produce nothing. Its sole power is that of affecting distribution under penalty of preventing production. This may put wealth or capital in the hands of the appropriator, by taking it from others; but can never bring it into existence.

Part IV — The Distribution of Wealth

Chapter 1 — The Meaning of Distribution

As has already been observed, the distribution of wealth in political economy does not include transportation and exchange. Nor yet is there any logical reason for treating exchange as a separate department in political economy, as is done by those writers who define political economy as the science which teaches of the laws which regulate the production, distribution and exchange of wealth. Transportation and exchange are properly included in production, being a part of the process in which natural objects are, by the exertion of human labor, better fitted to satisfy the desires of man.

Nor yet again is there any logical reason in the division of the field of the science of political economy for establishing other departments treating of the consumption of wealth or of taxation. Taxation is a matter of human law, while the proper subject of science is natural law. Nor does the science of political economy concern itself with consumption. It is finished and done — the purpose for which production began is concluded when it reaches distribution.

The need of a consideration of the distribution of wealth in political economy comes from the cooperative character of the production of wealth in civilization. In the rudest state of humanity, where production is carried on by isolated human units, the product of each unit would in the act of production come into possession of that unit, for there would be no distribution of wealth and no need for considering it. But in that higher state of humanity where separate units, each moved to action by the motive of satisfying its individual desires, cooperate to production, the question of distribution necessarily arises.

Distribution is in fact a continuation of production — the latter part of the same process of which production is the first part. For the desire which prompts to exertion in production is the desire for satisfaction, and distribution is the process by which what is brought into being by production is carried to the point where it yields satisfaction to desire — which point is the end and aim of production.

In a logical division of the field of political economy, that which relates to the distribution of wealth is the final part. For the beginning of all the actions and movements which political economy is called on to consider is in human desire. And their end and aim is the satisfaction of that desire. When this is reached political economy is finished, and this is reached with the distribution of wealth. With what becomes of wealth after it is distributed political economy has nothing whatever to do. It can take any further account of it only should it be reentered in the field of political economy as capital, and then only as an original and independent entry. What men choose to do with the wealth that is distributed to them may be of concern to them as individuals, or it may be of concern to the society of which they are a part, but it is of no concern to political economy. The branches of knowledge that consider the ultimate disposition of wealth may be instructive or useful. But they are not included in political economy, which does not embrace all knowledge or any knowledge, but has as a separate science a clear and well-defined field of its own.

If, moved by desire for potatoes, I dig, or plant, or weed, or gather them, or as a member of the great cooperative association in which civilization consists, I saw or plane, or fish or hunt, or play the fiddle, or preach sermons for the satisfaction of other people who in return will give me potatoes or the means of getting potatoes, the whole transaction originating in my desire for potatoes is finished when I get the potatoes, or rather when they are put at my disposal at the place contemplated in my desire. Whether I then choose to boil, bake, roast or fry them, to throw them at dogs or to feed them to hogs, to plant them as seed, or to let them decay; to trade them off for other food or other satisfactions, or to transfer them to someone else as a free gift or under promise that by and by he will give me other potatoes or other satisfactions, is something outside of and beyond the series of transactions which originating in my desire for potatoes was ended and finished in my getting potatoes.

As a term of political economy, distribution is usually said to mean the division of the results of production among the persons or classes of persons who have contributed to production. But this as we shall see is misleading, its real meaning being the division into categories corresponding to the categories or factors of production.

In entering on this branch of our inquiry, it will be particularly needful to keep in mind that the laws which it is the proper purpose of political economy to discover are not human laws, but natural laws. From this it follows that our inquiry into the laws of the distribution of wealth is not an inquiry into the municipal laws or human enactments which either here and now, or in any other time and place, prescribe or have prescribed how wealth shall be divided among men. With them we have no concern, unless it may be for purposes of illustration. What we have to seek are those laws of the distribution of wealth which belong to the natural order — laws which are a part of that system or arrangement which constitutes the social organism or body economic, as distinguished from the body politic or state, the Greater Leviathan that makes its appearance with civilization and develops with its advance. These natural laws are in all times and places the same, and though they may be crossed by human enactment, can never be anulled or swerved by it.

It is more needful to call this to mind, because in what have passed for systematic treatises on political economy the fact that it is with natural laws, not human laws, that the science of political economy is concerned, has in treating of the distribution of wealth been utterly ignored, and even flatly denied.

Chapter 2 — The Nature of Distribution

Mill's *Principles of Political Economy* is, I think, entitled to the rank of the best and most systematic exposition of the scholastically accepted political economy yet written, and as I wish to present in their very strongest form the opinions that I shall controvert, I quote Mill's argument from which it is assumed that the laws of distribution with which political economy has to deal are human laws.

> *The laws and conditions of the production of wealth, partake of the character of physical truths. There is nothing optional or arbitrary in them. Whatever mankind produce, must be produced in the modes and under the conditions imposed by the constitution of external things, and by the inherent properties of their own bodily and mental structure....*
>
> *But it is not so with the Distribution of Wealth. That is a matter of human institution solely. The things once there, mankind, individually or collectively can do with them as they like. They can place them at the disposal of whomsoever they please, and on whatever terms. Further, in the social state, in every state except total solitude, any disposal whatever of them can only take place by the consent of society, or rather of those who dispose of its active force. Even what a person has produced by his individual toil, unaided by anyone, he cannot keep, unless by the permission of society. Not only can society take it from him, but individuals could and would take it from him, if society only remained passive; if it did not either interfere en masse, or employ and pay people for the purpose of preventing him from being disturbed in the possession. The distribution of wealth, therefore, depends on the laws and customs of society. The rules by which it is determined are what the opinions and feelings of the ruling portion of the community make them, and are very different in different ages and countries; and might be still more different, if mankind so chose.*

The opinions and feelings of mankind, doubtless, are not a matter of chance. They are consequences of the fundamental laws of human nature, combined with the existing state of knowledge and experience, and the existing condition of social institutions and intellectual and moral culture. But the laws of the generation of human opinions are not within our present subject. They are part of the general theory of human progress, a far larger and more difficult subject of inquiry than political economy. We have here to consider, not the causes, but the consequences, of the rules according to which wealth may be distributed. Those, at least, are as little arbitrary, and have as much the character of physical laws, as the laws of production. Human beings can control their own acts, but not the consequences of their acts either to themselves or to others. Society can subject the distribution of wealth to whatever rules it thinks best; but what practical results will flow from the operation of those rules, must be discovered, like any other physical or mental truths, by observation and reasoning. We proceed, then, to the consideration of the different modes of distributing the produce of land and labor which have been adopted in practice or may be conceived in theory.

In all the dreary waste of economic treatises that I have plodded through, this, by a man I greatly esteem, is the best attempt that I know of to explain what is really meant in political economy by laws of distribution. And it is no small evidence of Mill's superiority to those who since the time of Adam Smith had preceded him, and to those who since his own time have followed him, in treatises which bear the stamp of authority in our schools and colleges, that he should feel it incumbent on him even to attempt this explanation. But this attempt brings into clear relief the unscientific character of what had passed and yet still passes as expositions of the science of political economy. In it we are deliberately told that the laws which it is the object of political economy to discover, are, in the first part of its inquiries, natural laws, but that in the later and practically more important part of these inquiries, they are human laws! Political economy of this sort is as incongruous as the image that troubled Nebuchadnezzar, with its head of fine gold and its feet part of iron and part of clay, for in the first part its subject-matter is natural law, and in the last and practically more important, it is human law.

Let us examine this argument carefully, for it is made on behalf of the current political economy by a man who from his twelfth year had been carefully trained in systematic logic and who before he wrote this had won the highest reputation as a logician.

The plausibility of the argument comes from the leading proposition — "The things once there, mankind individually or collectively can do with them as they like." It is evidently this that in the mind of Mill himself and in the minds of the professors and students who have since gone over his *Principles of Political Economy*, has seemed to prove beyond peradventure that though the laws of production may be natural laws, the laws of distribution are human laws. For in itself this proposition is a self-evident truth. Nothing, indeed, can be clearer than that "the things once there, mankind individually or collectively can do with them as they like" — that is to say, wealth once produced, human law may distribute it as human will may ordain.

Yet while this proposition — that things once there mankind can do with them as they like — is in itself irrefutable, the argument in which it is introduced is an egregious instance of the fallacy called by the logicians *petito principii*, or begging the question. The question that Mill is arguing is whether what is called in political economy the distribution of wealth is a matter of natural law or a matter of human law, and what he does is to cite the fact that in what human law calls the distribution of wealth, mankind can do as they like, and assume from that that the distribution of wealth in the economic sense of the term is a matter of human law — "a matter of human institution solely."

Such a fallacy could not have been proposed by Mill, himself a trained logician, nor could have passed current with the trained logicians who since his time, leaving their logic behind them, have written treatises on political economy, had it not been for the fact that in the scholastic political economy the real nature of the distribution of wealth has been slurred over and the question of what natural laws may have to do with it utterly ignored. Let us endeavor to settle this:

The original meaning of the word distribution is that of a division into or among. Distribution is thus an action, presupposing an exertion of will, and involving a power of giving that will effect. Now as to things already there, that is to say with wealth that has been already produced, it is perfectly clear that their division or distribution among men is determined entirely by human will backed by human force. With such a distribution nature is not concerned and in it she takes no part. Who shall possess or enjoy them is a matter purely of human will and force. Mankind can place them at the disposal of whomsoever they please and on whatever terms.

Thus, distribution in this sense, the distribution of things already in existence, is indeed a matter solely of human will and power. Where in civilized society it is human institutions that decide among whom wealth shall be divided, as for instance in the case of an insolvent, and the case of the estate of a deceased person, or in case of controverted ownership, the municipal law governing such distribution is to be found recorded in written or printed statutes, in the decisions of judges or in traditions of common use and wont. It is in cases of dispute authoritatively expounded by courts, and is carried into effect by sheriffs or constables or other officials having at their back the coercive power of the state, with its sanctions of seizure of property and person, fine, imprisonment and death.

But from its very rudest expression, where what obtains is

> *The good old rule,*
> *.... The simple plan,*
> *That they should take who have the power,*
> *And they should keep who can*

to societies with the most elaborate machinery for declaring and enforcing human laws of distribution, such laws always are and always must be based upon human will and human force.

How then can we talk of natural laws of distribution? Laws of nature are not written or printed, or carved on pillars of stone or brass. They have no parliaments, or legislatures, or congresses to enact them, no judges to declare them, no constables to enforce them. What then can we really mean by natural laws of the distribution of wealth? What is the mode or method by which wealth may be said to be distributed by natural law, without human agency, among individuals or classes of individuals? Here is the difficulty that, not having been cleared up in economic works, has given plausibility to the assumption into which the scholastic economy has fallen in assuming that the only laws of distribution with which political economy can deal are not natural laws at all, but only human laws — an assumption that must bring any science of political economy to an end with production.

Laws of nature, as was explained in the first part of this work, are the names which we give to the invariable uniformities of coexistence and sequence which we find in external things, and which we call laws of nature because our reason apprehends in them evidence of an originating will, preceding and superior to human will. Let us call in the aid of that most potent instrument of political economy, imaginative experiment, to see if we do not find evidences of such laws of nature, the only laws with which a true science of political economy can deal, in the matter of the distribution of wealth:

The shifting of desert sands reveals to a roving tribe wealth produced by a long dead civilization — rings, coins, bracelets, precious stones and delicately carved marbles. The things are there. They have been produced. The tribesmen individually or collectively can do with them as they like — and place them at the disposal of whomsoever they please, and on whenever terms. Nature will not interfere.

But things freshly produced this day or this minute are as truly here as things produced centuries ago. Why should not mankind individually or collectively do with them also as they like? They can do so with no more remonstrance from the things themselves or from external nature than would attend the rifling of Egyptian tombs by Bedouins. Why should not civilized men rifle the products of farm or mine or mill as soon as they appear? Human law interposes no objection to such collective action, for human law is but an expression of collective human will, and changes or ceases with changes in that will. Natural law, so far as it is comprehended in what we call physical law, interposes no objection — the laws of matter and energy in all their forms and combinations pay no heed whatever to human ownership.

Yet it needs no economist to tell us that if in any country the product of a living civilization were treated as the Bedouins treat the products of a dead civilization, the swift result would be fatal to that civilization — would be poverty, famine and death to the people individually and collectively. This result would come utterly irrespective of human law. It would make no difference whether the appropriation of "things once there" without regard to the will of the producer were in defiance of human law or under the sanction of human law; the result would be the same. The moment producers saw that what they produced might be taken from them without their consent, production would cease and starvation begin. Clearly then, this inevitable result is not a consequence of human law, but the consequence of natural law. Not a consequence of the natural laws of matter and motion, but a consequence of natural laws of a different kind — laws no less immutable than the natural laws of matter and motion.

For natural law is not all comprehended in what we call physical law. Besides the laws of nature which relate to matter and energy, there are also laws of nature that relate to thoughts and will. And should we treat the present products of farm or mine or mill or factory as we may treat the products of the dead civilization, we shall feel the remonstrance of an immutable law of nature wherever we come in conflict with the moral law. This is not to say that any division of wealth that mankind individually or collectively may choose to make will be interfered with or prevented. Things once here, once in existence in the present, are absolutely in the control of the men of the present, and "they can place them at the disposal of whomsoever they please and on whatever terms." A remonstrance of the moral law of nature to their action will not show itself in, or in relation to, these identical things. But it will show itself in the future — in checking or preventing the production of such things. Things on which the natural laws of distribution exert their control are not things already produced, but things which are being, or are yet to be, produced.

Production in political economy is not something which goes on for a while and then stops, when its product, wealth, has been brought into being; nor is it something related only to a production that is finished and done. Both production and distribution are properly conceived of as continuous, resembling not the drawing of water in a bucket but the drawing of water through a pipe — or better still, in the conveyance of water over an elevation by means of a bent pipe or siphon, of which the shorter arm may stand for production and the longer for distribution. It is in our power to tap this longer arm of the pipe at any point below the highest and take what water is already there. But the moment we do so, the continuity of the stream is at an end, and the water will cease to flow.

Production and distribution are in fact not separate things, but two mentally distinguishable parts of one thing — the exertion of human labor in the satisfaction of human desire. Though materially distinguishable, they are as closely related as the two arms of the siphon. And as it is the outflow of water at the longer end of the siphon that is the cause of the inflow of water at the shorter and, so it is that distribution is really the cause of production, not production the cause of distribution. In the ordinary course, things are not distributed because they have been produced, but are produced in order that they may be distributed. Thus interference with the distribution of wealth is interference with the production of wealth, and shows its effect in lessened production.

To use again the analogy supplied by our material frames: blood stands in the same relation to the physical body that wealth does to the social body, distributing throughout all parts of the physical frame potentialities akin to those which wealth carries to the social frame. But though the organs that distribute this vital current are different from the organs that produce it, their relations are so intimate that seriously to interfere with the distribution of the blood is necessarily to interfere with its production. Should we say of the blood that passes into the great pumping station, the heart, "it has been produced; it is here, and we may do with it as we please!" And acting on the word, diverted from its course through the organs of distribution — at once the great pump ceases to beat and the organs that produce blood lose their power and begin to decompose. And as to pierce the heart and divert the blood that has been produced from the natural course of its distribution is to bring about the death of the physical organism most swiftly and certainly, so to interfere with a natural laws of the distribution of wealth is to bring about a like death of the social organism. If we seek for the reason of ruined cities and dead civilizations we shall find it in this.

Chapter 3 — Physical and Moral Laws

Our will is free. But human will can only affect external nature by taking advantage of natural laws, which in the very name we give them carry the implication of a higher and more constant will. A boy may throw a stone or an artilleryman fire a cannon ball at the moon. If the result depended solely on the human action, both ball and stone would reach the moon. But the governance of natural law — without conformity to which even such action as throwing a stone or firing a cannon ball cannot take place — continuing to modify results, brings both to the ground again, the one in a few feet and the other in a few thousand feet.

And the natural laws which political economy discovers, whether we call them laws of production or laws of distribution, have the same proof, the same sanction and the same constancy as the physical laws. Human laws change, but the natural laws remain, the same yesterday, today and tomorrow; manifestations to us of a will that though we cannot obtain direct knowledge of it through the senses, we can yet see never slumbers nor sleeps and does not change in jot or tittle.

If I can prove that this inflexibility to human effort is characteristic of the laws of distribution that political economy seeks to discover, I have proved finally and conclusively that the laws of distribution are not human laws, but natural laws. To do this it is only necessary to appeal to facts of common knowledge.

Now the three great laws of distribution, as recognized by all economists, though they are sometimes placed in different order, are the law of wages, the law of interest and the law of rent. Into these three elements or factors, the entire result of production is by natural law distributed. Now I do not of course mean to say that human law may not take from the part which under the natural law of distribution might be enjoyed by one man or set of men and give it to another, for as I have already said all wealth or any wealth from the moment it is produced is entirely at the disposition of human law. What I mean to say is that human law is utterly powerless directly to alter distribution, so that the laborer as laborer will get more wages or less wages, the capitalist as capitalist more interest or less interest, or the landowner as landowner more rent or less rent, or in any way alter the conditions of distribution fixed by natural law under existing industrial conditions. This has been tried again and again by the strongest governments, and is to some extent still being tried, but always unavailingly.

There have been at various times attempts to regulate wages by law, sometimes to decrease them and sometimes to increase them below or above the level fixed at the time by natural law. But it was found that in the one case no law could prevent the labor from asking and the employer from paying more than this legal rate when the equation of demand and supply made wages higher, and that no law could in the opposite case keep wages at a higher rate. So it has proved with interest. There been numberless attempts to keep down interest, and the State of New York retains to this day a law limiting, though with considerable holes, the rate of interest to six percent. But such laws never have succeeded and do not now succeed in keeping interest below the natural rate. Lenders receive and borrowers pay that rate in the form of sales, premiums, discounts and bonuses, where the law forbids them to do it openly. So, too, in the case of rents. The British Parliament has recently attempted to reduce agricultural rent in certain cases in Ireland by instituting officials with power to fix "fair rents" — what should be paid by the tenant to the landlord. They have in many cases cut down the income of certain of the landlords, but they have not lessened rent. They have merely divided what before went to the landlord between him and the existing tenant, and a new tenant must pay, part in rent to the landlord and part in tenant right to the existing tenant, as much for the use of the land as it would have commanded if this attempt to reduce rent had not been made.

And so it has been with attempts of human law to fix and regulate prices, which involve the same great laws of distribution in combined forms. Human law is always potent to do as mankind will with what has been produced, but it cannot directly affect distribution. That it can reach only through production.

The distinction between the laws of production and the laws of distribution is not, as is erroneously taught in the scholastic political economy, that one set of laws are natural laws, and the other human laws. Both sets of laws are laws of nature. The real distinction is that the natural laws of production are physical laws and the natural laws of distribution are moral laws. And it is this that enables us to see in political economy more clearly than in any other science, that the government of the universe is a moral government, having its foundation in justice. Or, to put this idea in terms that fit it for the simplest comprehension, that the Lord our God is a just God.

In considering the production of wealth we are concerned with natural laws of which we can only ask what is, without venturing to raise the question of what ought to be. But the moment we turn from a consideration of the laws of the production of wealth to a consideration of the laws of the distribution of wealth the idea of ought or duty becomes primary. All consideration of distribution involves the ethical principle; it is necessarily a consideration of ought or duty — a consideration in which the idea of right or justice is from the very first involved.

Since the distribution of wealth is an assignment of ownership, the laws of distribution must be the laws which determine property in the things produced. Or to put it in another way, the principle which gives ownership must be the principle which determines the distribution of wealth. Thus what we may speak of in political economy as the law of property and the law of distribution are not merely laws of the same kind, springing from the same principle, but are in reality different expressions of the same fundamental law. Hence, in considering the origin and basis of property, we come again to the question, is it the law of nature or the laws of man that it is the office of the science of political economy to discover? To say that the distribution of wealth is "a matter of human enactment solely" is to say that property can have no other basis than human law; while to admit any basis of property in laws of nature is to say that the distribution of wealth is a matter of natural law.

Chapter 4 — Property

It is another evidence of the superiority of John Stuart Mill in logical acumen that he seems to have been the only one of the accredited economic writers who has recognized this necessary relation between the laws of distribution and the origin of property. From the introductory section of his book "Distribution," the section I have already quoted in full, he proceeds at once to a consideration of the origin of property, and indeed the first two chapters of the Book are entitled "Of Property."

But he is consistent in error. The same want of discrimination that leads him to treat distribution solely as a matter of human institution leads him to treat property solely as a matter of human institution. Hence, his consideration of property does not, as it should, help him to see the incongruity of the notion that while the laws of production are natural laws the laws of distribution are human laws; but gives to that error such seeming plausibility as one error may give to another. Contradictions and confusions are however as marked in his discussion of property as in his discussion of distribution:

> *Private property, as an institution, did not owe its origin to any of those considerations of utility, which plead for the maintenance of it when established. Enough is known of rude ages, both from history and from analogous states of society in our own time, to show, that tribunals (which always precede laws) were originally established, not to determine rights, but to repress violence and terminate quarrels. With this object chiefly in view, they naturally enough gave legal effect to first occupancy, by treating as the aggressor the person who first commenced violence, by turning, or attempting to turn, another out of possession. The preservation of the peace, which was the original object of civil government, was thus attained; while by*

> *confirming, to those who already possessed it, even what was not the fruit of personal exertion, a guarantee was incidentally given to them and others that they would be protected in what was so.*

All this I deny. It is in fact blank contradiction. Let the reader look over and consider it. In the first sentence we are told that private property did not originate in considerations of utility. In the second, that "tribunals (which always precede laws) were originally established, not to determine rights, but to repress violence and terminate quarrels." In the third, that they did this by treating as the aggressor the person who first commenced violence. In the fourth, that the preservation of the peace was the original object of such tribunals, and that by securing possession where there was no right they incidentally secured possession where there was right.

Thus, the first sentence asserts that private property did not originate in considerations of utility, and the three succeeding sentences that it did. For when all consideration of right is eliminated what remains as a reason for the preservation of the peace by the repression of violence and determination of quarrels, if not the consideration of utility? What Mill tells us is that society originally acted on the principle of the schoolmaster who says, "if I find any fighting I will not stop to ask the right or wrong, but will flog the boy who struck the first blow, for I cannot have the school thrown into disorder." If this is not a substitution of the principle of utility for the principle of right, what is it? And to this contradiction of himself, Mill adds that by confirming wrongful possession, society incidentally guarantees rightful possession! — something in the nature of things as impossible as that two railway trains should pass each other on a single track.

The fact is that Mill in his consideration of property is caught in the toils of that utilitarian philosophy which seeks to make the principle of expediency take the place of the principle of justice. Men can no more do this consistently than they can live without breathing, and Mill in his very attempt to base the institution of property on human law is driven despite himself into recognizing the moral law, and into talking of right and wrong, of ought and ought not, of just and unjust. Now these are terms which imply a natural law of morality. They can have no meaning whatever if expediency be the basis of property and human law its warrant.

The contradictions of this paragraph are shown through the whole consideration of property it introduces. While he strives to treat property solely as a matter of human institution, over and over again we find Mill forced to abandon his position and appeal to something superior to human institution — to right or justice.

Thus, in what follows the paragraph I have quoted, we find statements utterly contradictory of the notion that property has its origin in expediency and is determined by human enactment. In the very next section to that in which we are told that the origin of property is not in justice but in expediency, not in the desire to determine rights, but the desire to repress violence, we are told:

> *The social arrangements of modern Europe commenced from the distribution of property which was a result not of a just partition, or acquisition by industry, but of conquest and violence: and notwithstanding what industry has been doing for many centuries to modify the work of force, the system still retains many and large traces of its origin. The laws of property have never yet conformed to the principles on which the justification of private property rests. They have made property of things which never ought to be made property, and absolute property where only a qualified property ought to exist.*

Here we are told that, as a matter of fact, human laws of property did not originate in the expediency of repressing violence, but in violence itself; that they have never conformed to what we can only understand as the natural law of property, but have violated that natural law, by treating as property things that under it are not property. For to say that a human law ought to be different from what the legislature enacts is to say that there is a natural law by which human laws are to be tested. What indeed that natural law of property is by which all human enactments are to be tested, Mill a little later shows himself to be conscious of, for he says:

> *Private property, in every defense made of it, is supposed to mean the guarantee to individuals of the fruits of their own labor and abstinence.*

And this basis of a natural right of property — a right which is unaffected by and independent of all human enactments — is still further on even more definitely and clearly stated:

> *The institution of property, when limited to its essential elements, consists in the recognition, in each person, of a right to the exclusive disposal of what he or she have produced by their own exertions, or received, either by gift or by fair agreement, without force or fraud, from those who produced it. The foundation of the whole is, the right of the producers to what they themselves have produced.*

After thus conceding everything to natural law, Mill becomes concerned again for human law, and appeals to the "categorical imperatives" of Kant, the ought of moral law, to give sanction under certain circumstances to human law, declaring that:

> *Possession which has not been legally questioned within a moderate number of years, ought to be, as by the laws of all nations it is, a complete title.*

Then, recognizing for a moment the incongruity of making a legal possession — that is to say possession by virtue of human law — equivalent to possession by virtue of natural law, he continues:

> *It is scarcely needful to remark, that these reasons for not disturbing acts of injustice of old date, cannot apply to unjust systems or institutions; since a bad law or usage is not one bad act, in the remote past, but a perpetual repetition of bad acts, as long as a law or usage lasts.*

Now Mill himself has always spoken of property as a system or institution, which it certainly is. And he has just before stated that the existing systems or institutions of property have their source in violence and force, and therefore are certainly in his own view unjust and bad. Hence what he tells us here is in plain English that the sanction of prescription cannot be pleaded in defense of property condemned by the natural or moral law. This is perfectly true, but it is an utter contradiction of the notion that property is a matter of human law.

Chapter 5 — Cause of Confusion As To Property

Let us pause a moment before we go further in our examination of Mill's reasoning. What is it that so perplexes this trained logician and honestly minded man, involving him in such utter contradictions and confusions when he endeavors to trace the basis of property? It is evidently the same thing that has prevented all the scholastic economists, both those who preceded and those who have succeeded him, from giving any clear and consistent statement of the laws of distribution or of the origin of property. This is a pre-assumption that they cannot bring themselves to abandon — a pre-assumption that land must be included in the category of property and a place found in the laws of distribution for the income of landowners. Since natural law can take no cognizance of the ownership of land, they are driven in order to support this pre-assumption to treat distribution and property solely as matters of human institutions.

Mill, who though befogged by his utilitarian philosophy is in many respects the superior of all these writers, starts on his investigation of distribution and property with the same pre-assumption — with the same "string tied to his leg." He had been, as they have all been — from the really great Adam Smith to the most recent purveyors of economic nonsense in Anglo-German jargon — accustomed to regard property in land as the most certain, most prominent, most tangible, of all property — that which the lawyers call real property, and which in common speech is recognized as the highest expression of ownership. And his logic is not strong enough to permit him even at its call to lay rude hands upon what to Englishmen of his class and time was the most sacred of institutions. He did indeed, come so near questioning it as to excite the dismay of his contemporaries who deemed him a radical of radicals for utterances that squinted toward the truth. But he always draws back from uttering it.

The real basis of property, the real fundamental law of distribution, is so clear that no one who attempts to reason can utterly and consistently ignore it. It is a natural law which gives the product to the producer. But this cannot be made to cover property in land. Hence the persistent effort to find the origin of property in human law and its base in expediency. It is evident, even where Mill speaks of property generally, as he has done in what I have to this point commented on, that the real cause of his contradictions and confusions is that he has always in mind property in land. But the failure of the attempt to bring this species of property under the only possible justification of property, the right of the producer to the product, is even more painfully clear when he comes specifically to treat of it. He begins this by another admission of the truth utterly inconsistent with the derivation of property from expediency; saying:

> *Nothing is implied in property but the right of each to his (or her) own faculties....*
>
> *The essential principle of property being to assure to all persons what they have produced by their labor and accumulated by their abstinence, this principle cannot apply to what is not the produce of labor, the raw material of the earth.*

Abstinence is not a doing but a not doing, a refraining from consuming. The essential principle of property being to assure to all persons what they have produced by their labor, this of course includes what having been produced by labor is afterwards accumulated by abstinence. These words "and accumulated by their abstinence" are superfluous, but their introduction is significant of the disposition to assume that capital rather than labor is the active factor in production.

But though a little superfluous in phrase, this statement is true and clear. In the conflict going on in Mill's mind the perception of the basis of property and natural law seems, in the admission that the principle of property cannot apply to land, to have finally conquered both the notion that its basis is in human law and the pre-assumption from which the notion comes.

But this is hardly for a moment. In the next sentence, the pre-assumption that has confused him asserts its power and Mill proceeds to argue that the principle of property does apply to land. He does this by what is in reality, though doubtless unconsciously to him, a jumble with words. But as his argument is the stock argument of the scholastic economists, I will quote it in full, proceeding from the sentence already given:

> *If the land derived its productive power wholly from nature, and not at all from industry, or if there were any means of discriminating what is derived from each source, it not only would not be necessary, but it would be the height of injustice, to let the gift of nature be engrossed by individuals. The use of the land in agriculture must indeed, for the time being, be of necessity exclusive; the same person who has plowed and sown must be permitted to reap; but the land might be occupied for one season only, as among the ancient Germans; or might be periodically redivided as population increased; or the State might be the universal landlord, and the cultivators tenant under it, either on lease or at will.*
>
> *But though the land is not the produce of industry, most of its valuable qualities are so. Labor is not only requisite for using, but almost equally so for fashioning, the instrument. Considerable labor is often required at the commencement, to clear the land for cultivation. In many cases, even where cleared, its productiveness is wholly the effect of labor and art. The Bedford Level produced little or nothing until artificially drained. The bogs of Ireland, until the same thing is done to them, can produce little beside fuel... Cultivation also requires buildings and fences, which are wholly the produce of labor. The fruits of this industry cannot be*

reaped in a short period. The labor and outlay are immediate, the benefit is spread over many years, perhaps over all future time. A holder will not incur this labor and outlay when strangers and not himself will be benefited by it. If he undertake such improvements, he must have a sufficient period before him in which to profit by them; and he is in no way so sure of having always a sufficient period as when his tenure is perpetual.

These are the reasons which form the justification in an economical point of view, of property in land.

This argument begins by asserting that the principle of property cannot apply to land; it ends by asserting that it does. The language is loose, for Mill indulges in a practice dangerous where exactness is important, the use of paraphrases for economic terms, such as "raw material of the earth" and "gift of nature" for land; "industry" for labor, and "valuable qualities" for productive powers. But carefully to consider these reasons which are held to justify the unjustifiable, is to see that their plausibility is brought about in the same way that a juggler seems to change a watch into a turnip — the substitution of one thing for another while attention is distracted. In this case the substitution is of one sense of a word for another different sense of the same word.

The word land, as before explained, has two senses. One of these is that of the dry and solid superficies of the globe as distinguished from water or air, or that of the cultivable matter of the earth as distinguished from rock or sand or ice or bog. In this sense we frequently speak of "improved land" or "made land." The other, the economic sense of the word, is that of the natural or passive element in production, including the whole external world, with all its powers, qualities and products, as distinguished from the human or active element, labor, and its sub-element, capital. In this sense we cannot speak of "improved land" or "made land."

Such phrases would involve contradiction in terms.

Now in the reasoning just quoted Mill slips from one to the other of these two senses of the word land, not merely in the same connection, but in the same sentence, and even as between the noun and its pronoun without notice to the reader and seemingly without consciousness on his own part.

The first suggestion of this substitution comes in the ifs of the second sentence. If, says Mill, land derived its productive power wholly from nature and not at all from labor, or if there were any means of discriminating what is derived from each source, it would be the height of injustice to let land be engrossed by individuals.

Why these ifs? Mill is here writing as a political economist, in a work entitled *Principles of Political Economy,* and for the purpose in this particular place of discovering whether there is any justification from an economic point of view of property in land. Land, as a term of political economy, means that element of productive power derived from nature and not at all from labor. It has and can have no other meeting. The first principle of political economy is the distinction between the productive power derived wholly from nature, for which its term is land, and the productive power derived from human exertion, for which its term is labor. Where the reason can find no "means of discriminating what is derived from each source," political economy becomes impossible, and to confuse this discrimination is to abandon political economy.

This is precisely what Mill does, when he goes on in the first sentence of the next paragraph to tell us that "though land is not the produce of industry, most of its valuable qualities are so." He is abandoning political economy by dropping in the pronoun the sense in which he uses the word land in the noun, and falling with seeming unconsciousness into the vague sense of common speech. When he says that land is not the produce of industry he uses the word in the economic sense. But when he says the qualities of land are the produce of labor he is using the word in that loose ordinary sense in which we speak of "improved land". For what single quality of land in the economic sense of the word is the produce of labor? Is it gravitation? It it extension? Is it cohesion? Is it chemical affinities or repulsions? Is it the qualities shown in generation and germination and growth?

The fact is, that abandoning the economic sense of the word land, he resorts to that loose colloquial sense of the word in which we speak of "improving the land." And it is with illustrations of "improved land" and "made land" that he goes on to show how the qualities of land are products of labor.

Let me to do a little illustrating, for the confusions to which Mill succumbed are being crammed into the minds of young people by a thousand "professors of political economy":

I am writing these pages on the shore of Long Island, where the Bay of New York contracts to what is called the Narrows, nearly opposite the point where our legalized robbers, the Custom House officers, board incoming steamers to ask strangers to take their first American swear, and where if these false oaths really colored the atmosphere the air would be bluer than is the sky on this gracious day. I turn from my writing-machine to the window, and drink in, with a pleasure that never seems to pall, the glorious panorama.

"What do you see?" If in ordinary talk I were asked this, I should of course say, "I see land and water and sky, ships and houses and light clouds, and the sun, drawing to its setting, over the low green hills of Staten Island, and illuminating all."

But if the question referred to the terms of political economy, I should say, "I see land and wealth." Land, which is the natural factor of production; and wealth, which is the natural factor so changed by the exertion of the human factor, labor, as to fit it for the satisfaction of human desires. For water and clouds, sky sun, and the stars that will appear when the sun is sunk, are, in the terminology of political economy, as much land as is the dry surface of the earth to which we narrow the meaning of the word in ordinary talk. And the window through which I look; the flowers in the garden; the planted trees of the orchard; the cow that is browsing beneath them; the Shore Road under the window; those vessels that lie at anchor near the banks, and the little pier that juts out from it; the trans-Atlantic liner steaming through the channel; the crowded pleasure-steamers passing by; the fort and dwellings on the opposite side of the Narrows; the big wooden elephant of Coney Island; and the graceful sweep of the Brooklyn Bridge, that may be discovered from a little higher up; all alike fall into the economic term wealth — land modified by labor so as to afford satisfaction to human desires. All in this panorama that was before man came here, and would remain were he to go, belongs to the economic category land; while all that has been produced by labor belongs to the economic category wealth, so long as it retains its quality of ministering to human desire. But on the other shore, in view from the window, is a little rectangular piece of dry surface, evidently reclaimed from the line of water by filling in with rocks and earth. What is that? In ordinary speech it is land, as distinguished from water, and I should intelligibly indicate its origin by speaking of it as "made land." But in the categories of political economy there is no place for such a term as "made land." For the term land refers only and exclusively to productive powers derived wholly from nature and not at all from industry, and whatever is, and insofar as it is, derived from land by the exertion of labor, is wealth. This bit of dry surface raised above the level of the water by filling in stones and soil, is, in the economic category, not land, but wealth. It has land below it and around it, and the material of which it is composed has been drawn from land; but in itself it is, in the proper speech of political economy, wealth; just as truly as the ships I behold are not land but wealth, though they to have land below them and around them and are composed of materials drawn from land.

Now here is the evident confusion in Mill's thought, which he has perplexed by dropping from the terminology of political economy into the language of ordinary speech. The Bedford Level, which is land that has been drained; the cultivable bogs of Ireland, which is land that has a coating of soil put on it; the improved farms he refers to, which are land cleared or manured by labor, belong all of them to the same economic category as the little piece of "made land" visible from my window. In the qualities that he is considering in them they are all, in the economic meaning, not land at all, but wealth; not the free gift of nature, but the toil-earned produce of labor. In this, and so far as these qualities go, but no further — that is, insofar as they are wealth, not land, they are property; not because human agency can add any qualities to the natural factor, but because of the natural law of property, which gives to the producer the ownership of what his labor has produced.

Mill seems to think that he has shown the justification of property in land, but the reasons he gives only justify property in the produce of labor; thus in his own case adding a single instance of the truth of what he has before stated that "in every defense made of it, property is supposed to mean the guarantee to individuals of the fruits of their own labor."

Part V — Money: The Medium of Exchange and Measure of Value

Chapter 1 — Confusions as to Money

There is no social idea or instrument with which civilized men are more generally and personally familiar than money. From early infancy to latest age we all use it in thought and speech and daily transactions, without practical difficulty in distinguishing what is money from what is not money. Yet as to what it really is and what it really does, there are both in common thought on economic subjects and in the writings of professed economists the widest divergences.

The latest American cyclopedia (Johnson's, 1896) gives this definition: "Money is that kind of currency which has an intrinsic value, and which thus if not used as currency would still be wealth." Thus, there are some who say that money really consists of the precious metals, and whatever may be locally, temporarily or partially used as money can be so used only as a representative of these metals. They hold that the paper money which now constitutes so large part of the currency of the civilized world derives its value from the promise, expressed or implied, to redeem it in one or another of these metals, and by way of assuring such redemption vast quantities of these precious metals are kept widely in store by governments and banks.

On the other hand there are those who say that what makes a thing money is the edict or fiat of government that it shall be treated and received as money.

And again, there are others still who contend that whatever can be used in exchange to the avoidance of barter is money, thus including in the meaning of the term, notes, checks, drafts, etc., issued by private parties, as fully as the coins or notes issued by governments or banks.

Much of the contradiction and confusion which exists in popular thought proceeds from the pressure of personal interests brought into the question by the relation of debtor and creditor. But the confusions which prevail among professed economists have a deeper source. They evidently result from the confusions which prevail in economic thought and teaching as to the nature of wealth and the cause of value. Money is the common measure of value, the common representative and exchanger of wealth. Unless we have clear ideas of the meaning of value and the nature of wealth, it is manifest therefore that we cannot form clear ideas as to the nature and functions of money. But since we have cleared up in the preceding chapters the meaning of the terms value and wealth, we are now in a position to proceed with an inquiry into the nature, function and laws of money. It is unnecessary to waste time with any attempt to disentangle the maze of contradictory statements of fact and confusions of opinion with which the current literature of the subject is embarrassed. The true course of all economic investigation is to observe and trace the relation of those social phenomena that are obvious now and to us. For economic laws must be as invariable as physical laws. As the chemist or astronomer can safely proceed only from relations which he sees do here and now exist to infer what has existed or will exist, so it is with the political economist.

Yet we find, if we consider them, that these divergences in the definition of money spring rather from differences of opinion as to what ought to be considered and treated as money, than from differences as to what, as a matter of fact, money actually is. The men who differ most widely in defining money find no difficulty in agreeing as to what is meant by money in daily transactions. Since we cannot find a consensus of opinion among economists, our best plan is to seek it among ordinary people. To see what is usually meant by money we have only to know the essential characteristics of that which we all agree in treating as money in our practical affairs.

Chapter 2 — The Common Understanding of Money

When we are confused as to the true meaning of an economic term, our best plan is to endeavor to obtain a consensus of opinion as to what the thing really is; what function it really performs. After we have seen what money really is, and what functions it performs, we shall then be in a position to determine what are the best forms of money.

If I have agreed to pay money to another the common understanding of what money is will not hold my agreement fulfilled if I offer him wood, or bricks, or services, or gold or silver bullion, even though, as closely as can be estimated, these may be of equal value to the money promised. My creditor might take such things in lieu of what I had agreed to pay. But he would be more likely to object, and his objection, fully expressed, would amount to this: "What you agreed to pay me was money. With money I can buy anything that anyone has to sell, and pay any debt I owe. But what you offer me is not money. It is something I would be willing to take if I happened to have any personal use for it. But I have no personal use for it, and to get anyone to give me for it what I may want, I must find someone who wants this particular thing and make a trade with him. What you propose would therefore put on me trouble, risk and loss not contemplated in our agreement." And the justice of this objection would be recognized by all fair men.

In this — in the ease with which it may be passed from hand to hand in canceling obligations or transferring ownership — lies the peculiar characteristic of money. It is not the intrinsic nature of the thing, but the use to which it is applied that gives its essential character to money, and constitutes the distinction between it and other things. Even children recognize this. If I make friends with a little one of four or five, and, showing a stick of candy, ask "What is this for?" It will say, "That is to eat." If I show a hat or a pair of shoes, it will say, "That is to wear." But if I show a piece of money, it will say, "That is to buy things with."

Now, in this, the little child will give the definition of money that, whatever may be our monetary theories, we all practically recognize. The peculiar use of money — what money "is for" — is that of buying other things. What by virtue of this use is money, may or may not have capability for any other use. That is not material. For as long as a thing is reserved to the use of buying things, any use inconsistent with this use is excluded.

We might, for instance, put sticks of candy to the use of buying things. But the moment a stick of candy was applied to the use of being eaten, its use in buying things would end. So, if a greenback be used to light a cigar, its use as money is destroyed. Even where coins are used as ornaments, their use as money is during that time prevented.

In short, the use of money, no matter of what it be composed, is not directly to satisfy desire, but indirectly to satisfy desire through exchange for other things. We do not eat money nor drink money nor wear money. We buy other things with it. We esteem money and seek it, not for itself, but for what we may obtain by parting with it. This is true even where money is hoarded, for the gratification which hoarding gives is the consciousness of holding at command that with which we may readily buy anything we may wish to have.

The little child I have supposed would probably not know the meaning of the word exchange, which is that of the voluntary transfer of desired things for desired things. But it would know the thing, having become familiar with it in the little exchanges that go on between children — in the giving of marbles for candy or toys, or in transactions based on "I will do this for you, if you will do that for me." But such exchanges it would probably speak of as trades or swaps, reserving the words buying or selling to exchanges in which money is used.

In this use of words the child would conform to a practice that has become common among careful writers. Both in ordinary usage and in political economy we generally confine the words buying and selling to exchanges in which money is given or promised, speaking of an exchange in which money is not involved as a barter or trade, or simply an exchange. It is where money is one of the things exchanged that the transaction is called a purchase and a sale.

In this usage, we habitually treat money as though it were the more notable or more important side of exchanges in which things not money are given for money — that side of exchange from which or towards which the initiative impulse proceeds. And there is another usage which points in the same direction. Among the masses of our people at least, good manners is held to require that where money passes in a transaction of exchange, the receiver of the money should by some such phrase as "Thank you," indicate a sense of benefit or obligation.

The reason of both these usages is, I think, to be found in the fact that money is the thing in which gain or profit is usually estimated; the thing which can usually be most readily and certainly exchanged for any other thing. It is this that makes it seem to those who do not look closely, that what is sought in exchange is money, and that he who gets money in return for other things, is in a better position than he who gets other things in return for money.

To see in what money really differs from other things having exchangeable or purchasing power, let us imagine a number of men to undertake a journey through a country where they have no personal acquaintance. Let them for instance start from New York, in pleasant weather, to make a leisurely trip by the high road for two hundred miles. Let them for the defrayal of the expenses of the journey provide themselves with exchangeable things of different kinds. Imagine one to have a valuable horse; another some staple commodity, such as tobacco or tea; another gold and silver bouillon; another a check or bill of exchange, or a checkbook; and the fifth to have current money. These things might have value to the same amount, but at the first stop for rest and refreshment a great difference between them as to readiness of convertibility would be seen.

The only way the man with the horse could pay for the slightest entertainment for man or beast, without selling his horse for money, or bartering for things that might be very inconvenient to carry, would be by trading him for less valuable horse. It is clear that he could not go far in this way, for, to say nothing of the delays incident to horse trades, he would, if he persisted in them under pressure of his desire to go on, soon find himself reduced to an animal that could hardly carry itself.

Though of staple commodities, tobacco and tea are probably those most readily divisible and easily carried, the tourist who tried to pay his way with them would find much difficulty. If not driven to sell his stock outright for what money he could get, he would virtually have to convert his pleasure excursion into a peddling trip; and to say nothing of the danger he would run of being arrested for infringement of Federal or local license laws, would be put to much delay, loss and annoyance in finding those willing to give the particular things he needed for the particular things he had.

And while gold and silver are of all commodities those which have the most uniform and staple value, yet the man who had started with bullion would, after he had left the city, hardly find anyone who could tell their real value or was willing to take them in return for commodities or service. To exchange them at anything like a reasonable rate he would have to hunt up some village jeweler who could test and weigh them, and who, though he might offer to give him a clockwork trinket, or to repair his watch in exchange, would hardly have the commodities or service our traveler needed at his disposal. To get what he wanted for what he had to give without recourse to money he would be driven to all sorts of intermediate exchanges.

As for the man with the checkbook, or check or bill of exchange, he would find himself the worst of all. He could make no more use of them where he was not known than of so much blank paper, unless he found someone who could testify to his good credit or who would go to the expense of telegraphing to learn it. To repeat this at every stopping-place, as would be necessary if his trip were to be carried through as it had been begun, would be too much for the patience and endurance of an ordinary man.

But the man with the money would find no difficulty from first to last. Everyone who had any commodity to exchange or service to render would take his money gladly and probably say "thank you" on receiving it. He alone could make the journey he set out to make, without delay or annoyance or loss on the score of exchanges.

What we may conclude from this little imaginative experiment is not that of all things money is the most valuable thing. That, although many people have in a vague way accepted it, would involve a fallacy of the same kind that is involved in the assumption that a pound of lead is heavier than a pound of feathers. What we may safely conclude from our experiment is, that of all exchangeable things money is the most readily exchangeable, and indeed that this ready exchangeability is the essential characteristic of money. Yet we have but to extend our illustration so as to imagine our travelers taking with them beyond this country that same money that they found so easily exchangeable here, to see that money is not one substance, nor in all times and places the same substance. What is money in the United States is not money in England. Although in places in each country much resorted to by travelers from another country, the money of the two countries may circulate together, as American money with English money in Bermuda; or Canadian money with American money at Niagara Falls; yet the traveler who wishes to pass beyond such monetary borders with what will readily exchange for the things he may need must provide himself with the money of the country. The money that has served him in the country he has left becomes in the country using a different money a mere commodity the moment he leaves the monetary border, which he will find it advantageous to exchange with some dealer in such commodities for money of the country.

Is money therefore a matter of mere governmental regulation? That is to say, can governmental statute or fiat, as is today contended by many, prescribe what money shall be used and at what rate it shall pass?

It is unnecessary for those of us who lived in or visited California between the years of 1862 and 1879, to look further than our own country and time to see that it cannot. During those years, while the money of the rest of the Union was a more or less depreciated paper, the money of that state and of the Pacific coast generally, was gold and silver. The paper money of the central government was used for the purchase of postage stamps, the payment of internal revenue dues, the satisfaction of judgments of the federal courts, and of those of the state courts where there was no specific contract, and for remittances to the East. But between man and man, and in ordinary transactions, it passed only as a commodity.

If it be said that governmental power was not fully exerted in this case; that the United States government dishonored its own currency in making bonds payable and Custom House dues receivable only in gold, and that the California specific contract law virtually gave the recognition of the State courts only to gold and silver, it may turn to such examples as that of the Confederate currency; as that of the Continental currency; it as that afforded by Colonial currencies prior to the Revolution, or as that of the French *assignats.*

Government may largely affect the use of money, as it may largely affect the use of language. It may enact what money shall be paid out and received by government officials, or recognized in the courts, as it may prescribe in what language government documents shall be printed or legislative or legal proceedings held, or scholars in the public schools be taught. But it can no more prescribe what shall be used as the common medium of exchange between man and man in transactions that depend on mutual consent than it can prescribe in what time mothers shall teach their babies to lisp. In all the many efforts that governments, limited or absolute, have made to do this, the power of government has signally failed.

Shall we say then, as do many who point out this impotency of mere government fiat, that the exchange value of any money depends ultimately upon its intrinsic value; that the real money in the world, the only true and natural money, is gold and silver?

This notion is even more widely opposed to facts then is that of the fiatists. Gold and silver have for the longest time and over the widest area served, and yet do serve, as material for money, and sometimes have served, and in some places yet do serve, as money. This was the case to some extent, in the early days of the California diggings, when every merchant or hotel-keeper or gambler or bartender was provided with a bottle of acid and a pair of scales, and men paid for goods or food or lodging or drinks or losses out of buckskin bags in which they carried gold dust or nuggets. But gold and silver are not the money of the world. The traveler who should attempt to go round the world paying his expenses with gold and silver bullion would meet great difficulty. Nor would he obviate that difficulty by taking instead of bullion, gold and silver coin. The truth is that there is no universal money and never yet has been, any more than there is or has been, in times of which we have knowledge, a universal language.

As for intrinsic value, it is clear that our paper money, which has no intrinsic value, performs every office of money — is in every sense as truly money as our coins, which have intrinsic value; and that even of our coins, their circulating or money value has for the most part no more correlation to intrinsic value than it has in the case of our paper money. And this is the case today all over the civilized world

The fact is that neither the fiat of government nor the action of individuals nor the character or intrinsic value of the material used, nor anything else, can make money or mar money, raise or lessen its circulating value, except as it affects the disposition to receive it as a medium of exchange.

In different times and places all sorts of things capable of more or less easy transfer have been used as money. Thus in San Francisco in the early days, when the sudden outflow of gold from the mines brought a sudden demand for money which there was no ready means of supplying, bogus coins, known to be bogus, passed from hand to hand as money. In New York at the beginning of the Civil War, when there was a great scarcity of circulating medium, owing to the withdrawal of gold and silver from circulation, postage stamps, car tickets, bread tickets, and even counterfeit notes, known to be counterfeit, passed from hand to hand as money.

Shall we say then that they are right who contend that a true definition of money must include everything that can be used in exchange to the avoidance of barter?

Clearly, we cannot say this, without ignoring a real and very important distinction — the distinction between money and credit.

For a little consideration will show that the checks, drafts, negotiable notes and other transferable orders and obligations which so largely economize the use of money in the commercial world today, do so only when accompanied by something else, which money itself does not require. That something else is trust or credit. This is the essential element of all devices and instruments for dispensing with the mediumship of money without resort to barter. It is only by virtue of it that they can take the place of the money.

When I give money for what I have bought, I pay my debt. The transaction is complete. But I do not pay my debt when I give a check for the amount; I merely give an order on someone else to pay in my place. If he does not, I am still responsible in morals and in law. And as a matter of fact no one will take a check of mine unless he trusts or credits me. And though an honest face, good clothes and a manifest exigency might enable me to pass a small check upon one who did not know me, without the guarantee of someone he did know, I could as readily, and perhaps more readily, get him to trust me outright. So, I cannot, except to one who knows me or to whom I am identified as a man of good credit, pass the check of another or his note or draft or bill of exchange in my favor, and without guaranteeing it by endorsement. Even then I do not make a payment; I merely turn over with my own guarantee an order for the payment.

Thus there is a quality attaching to money, in common apprehension, which clearly distinguishes it from all forms of credit. It is, so far as the giver of the money is concerned, a final closing of the transaction. For money is properly recognized by municipal law as the common medium of exchange.

All such things as checks, drafts, notes, etc., though they largely dispense with and greatly economize the use of money, do so by utilizing credit. Credit as a facilitator of exchange is older than money and perhaps is even now more important than money, though it may be made into money, as gold may be made into money. But though it may be made into money, it is not in itself money, any more than gold of itself is money, and cannot, without confusion as to the nature and functions of money, be included as money.

What then shall we say that money is?

Evidently the essential quality of money is not in its form or substance, but in its use.

Its use being not that of being consumed, but of being continually exchanged, it participates in and facilitates other exchanges as a medium or flux, serving upon a larger scale the same purpose of keeping tally and facilitating transfers as is served by the chips or counters often used in games of chance.

This use comes from a common or usual consent or disposition to take it in exchange, not as representing or promising anything else, but as completing the exchange

The only question anyone asks himself in taking money in exchange is whether he can, in the same way, pass it on in exchange. If there is no doubt of that, he will take it; for the use he has for money is to pass it on in exchange. If he has doubt of that, he will take it only at a discount proportioned to the doubt, or not take it at all.

What then makes anything money is the common consent or disposition to accept it as a common medium of exchange. If a thing has this essential quality in any place and time, it is money in that place and time, no matter what other quality it may lack. If a thing lacks this essential quality in any place and time, it is not money in that place and time, no matter what other quality it may have. To define money:

Whatever in any time and place is used as the common medium of exchange is money in that time and place.

2. Common Understanding of Money

There is no universal money. While the use of money is almost as universal as the use of languages, and it everywhere follows general laws as does the use of languages, yet as we find language differing in time and place, so do we find money differing. In fact, as we shall see, money is in one of its functions a kind of language — the language of value.

Chapter 3 — Medium of Exchange and Measure of Value

The primary quality of money is in its use as the common medium of exchange. But proceeding from this use as a common medium of exchange, money has another and closely conjoined use — that of serving as a common measure of value.

The reason of this is that the use of money as a common medium of exchange, which causes it to be esteemed for exchange and not for consumption, makes it of all exchangeable things that which in civilized society is most often and most commonly exchanged. A given portion of wood or coal, for instance, may be used by the producer and thus not be exchanged at all; or it may be exchanged once or perhaps even half a dozen times between cutting or mining and its reaching the consumer. So it is with potatoes or wheat or corn. The majority of horses are probably not exchanged at all during their working days, and it would be a much exchanged horse who could have six owners during his life. Cotton and wool and hemp and silk may pass from one to half a dozen exchanges before they assume the form of cloth or rope, and in that form pass through from two to half a dozen more exchanges before reaching the consumer. And so with lumber or iron or most of the forms of paper, meat or leather. Not only is the ultimate purpose of the exchanges of such things destructive consumption, but they are mainly composed of things which if not soon consumed would wear out or decay.

Money, on the other hand, is not produced for the purpose of being consumed, but for the purpose of being exchanged. This, not consumption, is its use. And we seek for its substance materials least subject to wear and decay, while it is usually carefully guarded by whoever for the moment may possess it. And further while an article of money may frequently pass through more hands in a single day than ordinary articles of wealth are likely to pass through during the whole of their existence, the use of money in thought and speech as a symbol of value brings it to the constant notice of those who do not often tangibly use it. Thus it is that the value of the money — the common medium of exchange in any community — becomes to the people of that community better known than the value of anything else, and hence is most readily and constantly chosen to compare the value of other things.

But here may arise a question, which I wish thoroughly to answer: if, as explained previously, value is in itself a relation to labor, why can we not find not merely a common measure of value, but an exact and final measure of value in labor itself?

This is a question that perplexes a great many of the monetary theories that have been broached in the United States. Yet in the light of our previous investigation the reason why the real measure of value cannot serve as a common measure of value is clear. It lies in the human constitution. We become conscious of exertion through the "toil and trouble" it involves — the feeling of effort and at length of irksomeness and repugnance that attends its continuance. Now feeling is an affection or condition of the individual perception or Ego, which can find objective manifestation only through action. Even a mother can know the feelings of her baby only through its actions. If she can tell that it is hungry or sleepy or in pain, or is satisfied and happy, it is only in this way.

As we have seen, labor, in the sense of exertion, is the true, ultimate and universal measure of value; what anything will bring in exchange is always based upon an estimate of the toil and trouble attendant upon the exertion which the possession of the thing will save.

While exertion is always the real measure of value, to which all common measures of value must refer, yet to get a common measure of value, which will enable us to express from one to another both quantity and quality (duration and intensity) of exertion, we must take some result of exertion, just as to find a common measure of heat, light, expansive force or gravitation we must take some tangible manifestation of those forms of energy. It is because commodities, being the results of exertion, are tangible manifestations of exertion that they are generally and naturally used as common measures of value.

Even where exertion is expressed in time, there is always at least an implied reference to accomplishment or results. On going ashore in San Francisco, a shipmate of mine, who could not tell a scythe from a marlinspike, hired out to a farmer in haying-time for five dollars a day. At his first stroke with the scythe he ran it so deep in the ground that he nearly broke it in getting it out. Though he indignantly denounced such antiquated tools as out of fashion, declaring that he was used to the "patent scythes that turn up at the end," he did not really feel wronged that the farmer would not pay him a cent, as he knew that the agreement for a day's labor was really an agreement for so much mowing.

In fact, the form of measuring exertion by time, at bottom, involves its measurement by result.

In short, while exertion, including both quantity and intensity, is always the true and final measure of value, it is only through the manifestations of exertion that any common measure of value can be had. Thus commodities, being tangible expressions of exertion, become the readiest common measures of value, and have since the beginning of human society been so used.

While any commodity, or for that matter any definite service, may be used as a common measure of value, the tendency is always to use for this purpose the commodity whose value is most generally and easily recognized. And since the commodity which is used as the common medium of exchange becomes in that use the commodity which is oftenest exchanged and whose value is most generally and easily recognized, whatever serves as the common medium of exchange tends in that to become the common measure of value, in terms of which the values of other things are expressed and compared. In societies which have reached a certain stage of civilization this is always money. Hence we may define money with regard to its functions as that which in any time and place serves as the common medium of exchange and the common measure of value.

It must be remembered, however, that of these two functions, use as the common medium of exchange is primary. That is to say, use as the common medium of exchange brings about use as the common measure of value, and not the reverse.

But it is still evident, as Adam Smith said, that labor (in the sense of exertion) is "the real measure of the exchangeable value of all commodities," — "the only universal as well as the only accurate measure of value, or the only standard by which we can compare the values of all commodities in all times and in all places." For it is still true, as he said, that "the real price of everything, what everything really costs to the man who wants to acquire it, is the toil and trouble of acquiring it. What everything is really worth to the man who has acquired it, and wants to dispose of it or exchange it for something else, is the toil and trouble which it can save to himself, and which it can impose upon other people."

Since labor is thus the real and universal measure of value, whatever any country may use as a common measure of value can impose little difficulty upon the exchanges of its people with the people of other countries using other common measures of value. Nor yet would any change within a country from one common measure of value to another common measure of value bring more than slight disturbance were it not for the effect upon credits or obligations. In this lies the main source of the controversies and confusions with which the "money question" is now beset.

Before going further it would therefore be well, at least so far as pertains to the idea of money, to examine the relations of credit to exchange.

Chapter 4 — The Office of Credit in Exchanges

Imagine a number of shipwrecked men swimming ashore in their buffs to an uninhabited island in a climate genial enough to enable them to support life. What would be their first exchanges? Would they not be based upon the various forms of the proposition, "I will do or get this for you, if you will do or get this for me?" Now, no matter where or how they got into this world, this must have been the position of the first men when they got here, and all that we can reason from with any certainty goes to show that these first men must have been essentially the same kind of men as we ourselves.

If there is any difference in priority between them, credit must, in the nature of things, have preceded barter as an instrument of exchange, and must at least from the very first have assisted barter. What more natural than that the first man who had killed a deer, or made a large catch of fish, should be willing to give now, while he had abundance, in return for a promise that his neighbor would remember him in the same way when similarly fortunate? The organization of credit into more elaborate and finer forms goes on with the development of civilization, but credit must have begun to aid exchanges with the very beginning of human society, and it is in the backwoods and new settlements rather than in the great cities that we will today find its direct forms playing relatively the most important part in exchanges.

In explaining the origin and use of money, Adam Smith much overrated the difficulties of barter, and in this he has been followed by nearly all the writers who have succeeded him. Of the condition before the use of metals as money he says:

> *One man, we shall suppose, has more of a certain commodity than he himself has occasion for, while another has less. The former consequently would be glad to dispose of, and the latter*

> *to purchase, a part of this superfluity. But, if this latter should chance to have nothing that the former stands in need of, no exchange can be made between them. The butcher has more meat in his shop than he himself can consume, and a brewer and baker would each of them be willing to purchase part of it. But they have nothing to offer in exchange, except different productions of their respective trades, and the butcher is already provided with all the bread and beer which he has immediate occasion for. No exchange can, in this case, be made between them. He cannot be their merchant nor they his customers; and they are all of them thus mutually less serviceable to one another.*

Though this explanation of the difficulties attending barter has been paraphrased by writer after writer since Adam Smith, it is an exaggeration so gross as to be ridiculous. The differentiation of such trades as that of the butcher, brewer and baker, the fact that men habitually devote their labor to the production of more of certain commodities than they themselves can consume, implies a division of labor that could not possibly take place were exchange impossible under the circumstances that Adam Smith assumes. And it is evident that such circumstances would impose no insuperable difficulty to exchange even though a true money had not yet come into use. The butcher, with meat that he wanted to dispose of, would not have refused the exchange offered by the brewer and baker because he himself was already provided with all the bread and beer that he had immediate occasion for. On the contrary, he would say, "I have no immediate use for bread and beer because I am already supplied, but I will give you the meat you want on your promise to give me its equivalent in bread and beer when I call for them." Nor need he necessarily wait for his own supply of bread and beer to be exhausted before calling on the baker and brewer for the fulfillment of their promises, for since man's wants are not satisfied with meat, bread and beer alone, he might want from the tailor a coat, from the grazier a bullock, from the carpenter a house; and since they cannot take from him at once full payment in such a perishable commodity as meat, he could help out his part of the exchange by telling the baker and brewer to give to them the bread and beer they had promised him.

And that is to say, it is not necessary to an exchange that both sides of it shall be effected at once or with the same person. One part or side of the full exchange may be effected at once, and the effecting of the other part or side may be deferred to a future time and transferred to another person or persons by means of trust or credit. And by this simple and natural device, and without the intervention of money, salt could be exchanged for less quantities of beef or mutton than are likely to spoil before a single family could consume them. The truth is that the difficulties of barter, which Adam Smith speaks of here as if they were insuperable, are always avoided by the use of trust where trust is possible. It is really in exchange between those who are unknown to each other and do not expect to meet other again that money performs its most indispensable office. The use of money, by which the traveler can easily carry with him the means of supplying his needs, has greatly facilitated traveling; yet in the bill of exchange, the letter of credit, cook's coupons, and the book of certified checks, which are so largely displacing money for the use of travelers, we come back again to the use of trust.

Trust or credit is indeed the first of all the instrumentalities that facilitate exchange. Its use antedates not merely the use of any true money, but must have been coeval with the first appearance of man. Truth, love, sympathy are of human nature. It is not only that without them man could never have emerged from the savage state, but that without them he could not have maintained himself even in the savage state. If brought on earth without them, he would inevitably have been exterminated by his animal neighbors or have exterminated himself.

And trust or credit is not merely the first of the agencies of exchange in the sense of priority; it yet is, as it always has been, the first in importance. In spite of our extensive use of money in effecting exchanges, what is accomplished by it is small compared with what is accomplished by credit. In international exchanges money is not used at all, while the great volume of domestic exchange is in every civilized country carried on by the giving and cancellation of credits. As a matter of fact the most important use of money today is not as a medium of exchange, though that is its primary use. It is that of a common measure of value, its secondary use. Not only this, but with the advance in civilization the tendency is to make use of credit as money; to coin, as it were, trust into currency, and thus to bring into use a medium of exchange better adapted in many circumstances to easy transfer than metallic money. The paper money so largely in use in all civilized countries is in reality a coinage of credit or trust.

Chapter 5 — The Genesis of Money

Money is not an invention, but rather a natural growth or development, arising in the progress of civilization from common perceptions and common needs. The same fundamental law of human nature which prompts to exchange, the law by which we seek to satisfy our desires with the least exertion, prompts us with the growth of exchanges to adopt as a medium for them the most labor-saving instruments available.

All exchange is of services or commodities. But as commodities are, in reality, concrete services, they afford from the first the readiest media of exchange, performing that office and serving as measures of value not only for other commodities but for direct services.

In primitive societies, or any outposts of civilization where better means were not readily obtainable, skins, shells, salt, beads, tobacco, tea, blankets, and many other commodities have been used as common media of exchange and common measures of value, thus becoming the money of the time and place. But the metals, and particularly the precious metals, so will fill all the requirements of a medium of exchange, that wherever they have become well known mankind have applied them to this use. At first they were doubtless weighed, and perhaps tested, with every passage from hand to hand; but as their use for purposes of exchange became more common, the desire to economize labor must soon have led to the running of the metals into pieces of definite weight and purity, so that they may be passed from hand to hand without trouble of weighing and testing them. To make these pieces of circular form, and to afford evidence that they yet retained their original substance by stamping their sides and edges, are obvious devices that seem to have been adopted wherever sufficient skill in the arts had been attained and the metals were in this way used.

And thus by a natural development in use, a commodity peculiarly adapted to the purpose becomes, in the shape of coined money, the commodity which serves as a medium of exchange and measure of value for all commodities and services.

But while the first purpose of coinage is, we may safely assume, to save the trouble of weighing and testing the commodity which has become a common medium of exchange, the general use of these coins as giving evidence of weight and purity must gradually have the effect of transferring the quality of ready exchangeability from the commodity to the coin. The habit of weighing and testing passes away; even the amount of the commodity embodied in the coin is, by the great majority of those who use it, forgotten or not heeded; and the shape, size, color and devices on the coins become the things that give its circulation. An American Eagle, or ten-dollar piece, contains so many grains of gold of a certain fineness, and exchanges at the value of the gold. A man with a ten-dollar gold piece will find no difficulty in the United States in fairly exchanging it for anything he may happen to want, but he would find much difficulty in fairly exchanging the same quantity of gold in the shape of dust or of an ingot, anywhere except with a bullion dealer.

A curious evidence of this tendency to accept the sign rather than the substance is given in the history of the American trade dollar. For many years much of the export of silver to China has been in the shape of Mexican dollars, the stamp of which has become known there as evidencing a certain weight of silver. Thinking that it might take the place in China of the Mexican coin, the American government in 1874 coined what was called a trade dollar. It was better finished and handsomer than the Mexican dollar, and contained a greater weight of silver. But the Chinese preferred a coin whose look they had become familiar with, to one that was new to them, even though the latter was of greater intrinsic value. The attempt was a failure, and the coinage of the trade dollar was stopped.

Now this transfer of ready exchangeability from the commodity to the coin, with the accompanying relegation of the commodity itself to the same position in exchange held by other commodities, which takes place as a result of the use of coin money, is a matter of great importance, leading ultimately to a complete change in the nature of the money used.

In the coinage of the precious metals the use of commodities as a medium of exchange seems to have reached its highest form. But the very same qualities which of all commodities best fit the precious metals for this use, attach or may attach in still higher degree to something which, having no material form, may be passed from person to person or place to place without inconvenience from bulk or weight, or danger of injury from accident, abrasion or decay. This something is credit or obligation. And as the advance of civilization goes on, the same tendency to seek the gratification of desire with the least exertion, which with a certain advance of civilization leads to the development of commodity money, leads with its further advance to the utilization of credit as money.

Movement in this direction may be distinguished along three lines: 1) the admixture in coinage of obligation value with production value; 2) the use of obligation or credit as representing and economizing commodity money; 3) the use of pure credit money.

We are here considering only money. Not only is credit a facilitator of exchange before money of any kind is developed, but the same social progress which shows itself in the development of money also shows itself in the extension of credit. If the use of money supersedes the use of credit in some exchanges, it is only where the use of credit is difficult and inconvenient; and in facilitating exchanges over wider areas than the use of the primitive forms of credit would have been equal to, it also increases that mutual knowledge and mutual desire to exchange that are necessary to the extension of credit. Although the primary and local function of money is that of affording a common medium of exchange, its secondary function of affording a common measure of value soon becomes more important, and the extension of credit in our modern civilization is far more striking and important than the extension in the use of money as a medium of exchange. Though the use of any particular money as a medium of exchange is still local, the money of any one country circulating only to a very limited extent in other countries, yet the development of credit has been such that the exchange of commodities to the ends of the earth and among peoples using different moneys, is conducted by means of it. But what we are considering now is not this development of commercial credits, but the way in which the use of commodity money passes into the use of credit money; or in other words, the way in which the coinage of production value into a convenient medium of exchange passes into the coinage of obligation values.

The demand for any metal in exchange is, at first, like the demand for other things in exchange, a demand for consumption; and its value or rate of exchange is determined by the cost of producing it in merchantable form. As one or another of the metals began to come into use as a medium of exchange, the largest demand for it would doubtless for some time still be for consumption, and thus the value of the metal used as money would at first be no greater than that of the same metal intended for consumption. But when coinage fairly began, something more of labor would be required to produce the stamped and finished coin than to produce the mere ingot of merchantable shape.

Hence there are, or may be, two elements in the exchange value of metal coin — 1) the intrinsic value, or value of the metal itself, which is governed by the cost of producing it in merchantable form; and 2) the cost of changing it from that form into the form of finished coin. This second element, the charge for coinage, is called seignorage, from the idea that the coining of money has from the earliest times been deemed a function of the sovereign — the seignor or lord — as representative of organized society or the state.

Now the conversion of metal into coin seems always to have been paid for in the same way as the conversion of grain into meal or flour, by a toll or deduction in the return. This toll or seignorage may be less or more than the actual cost of coinage. It is what the lord or state, who has the sole privilege of coinage, chooses to take for it; the difference between the rate at which metal is received or bought at the mint and the rate at which it is returned or issued in coin.

Had the coinage of metal into money been left to the free competition of individual enterprise, the charge for this conversion would have tended to the lowest point at which coin could be produced in sufficient quantities to supply the demand. But so far as we can see this has never been the case. The primary object of coinage being the certification of weight and fineness, that is obviously best assured by the stamp of the highest and most widely known authority, that of the sovereign or state. Where coinage is thus monopolized in the hands of the sovereign, the element of seignorage in the value of coin may be eliminated altogether by the agreement or practice of the sovereign to return in coin the full amount of metal brought to his mint, as is today the case in some countries with some metals; or it may be extended so as to become the most important of the two elements in the value of coin by the refusal of the sovereign to coin on other terms and the exclusion or refusal of other coinage. Indeed, by the selection of some very cheap commodity for the material of coinage, it may become practically the only element of value. For, as Ricardo pointed out, the whole exchange value of paper money may be considered as a charge for seignorage.

The reason of this fact that, the issuance of money being a monopoly, the element of intrinsic value may be partially or entirely eliminated without loss of usefulness, is to be found in the peculiar use of money. The use of other commodities is in consumption. The use of money is in exchange. Thus the intrinsic character of money is of no moment to him who receives it to circulate again. The only question that he is concerned with is as to the readiness of others to receive it from him when he wants in his turn to pass it on. And this readiness where coin money comes into use as a common medium of exchange is associated with coinage, which becomes the badge or stamp of circulation.

Now the first coined money being commodity money, the demand for it would be for a long time, in part at least, a demand for consumption. In the simpler stage of the arts, coin would be much more frequently than now beaten or melted into plate, adornments, ornaments, etc. And more important still perhaps, it would continue to be used as a commodity in the exchange with other countries. It is probable that the coinage of the more important sovereigns had a far wider area of diffusion when international commerce was much less than it is now. For, although the area of commerce was more limited than now, there was proportionately more of the area without any coinage of its own, and before the widespread development of credit as a medium of international exchanges, the use of coin in them as a conveniently portable commodity was probably greater than now.

Now, the demand for coin sent abroad, as American gold sent to England, like the demand for coin for use in the arts, is a demand for use in consumption and would quickly show itself in a lessening of the aggregate demand and consequently of value, upon a reduction of the commodity value of coin, no matter how strictly the workmen of the mints were sworn to secrecy, as was the device of sovereigns who contemplated deteriorating their coinage.

But still more important is the fact that in order to keep up the value of coin while diminishing its intrinsic value it is necessary that the supply be strictly limited. But the sovereigns, whether princes or republics, who have resorted to the expedient of debasing their coinage have generally done so for the purpose of turning the same amount of metal into more coin, rather than that of keeping the same amount of coin in circulation with the use of less metal, or have been unable to resist the temptation to do this when they found opportunity.

Thus to the ministers and advisers of the sovereigns, who seem everywhere to have assumed from the first exclusive privilege of coining, it must have seemed an easy and safe economy to reduce the cost of the coin by substituting for its material some part of cheaper metal. Hence came those numerous and repeated reductions in the value of coins which are a marked feature in all monetary history; which have reduced the English pound sterling to but a fraction of its original equivalence to a pound troy, and in other countries have brought about a still greater difference.

So far as the principal and most important coinage is concerned, these attempts have from time to time ended in disaster, and in the final reunion of circulating value with commodity value, either by the rejection and withdrawal of the debased coin and a recoinage, or more frequently by the lowering of the circulating value to the level of the commodity value.

This, however, is not a necessary result of the debasement of coinage, as is so often assumed. A less valuable metal may be substituted in a coin for a more valuable metal without lessening the circulating value, provided — and this is the essential condition — it continues to be as hard for those who use the coin in exchanges to get the one as it was to get the other; or in other words that it continues to represent the same exertion.

For all exchange is really the exchange of labor, and the rate at which all things tend to exchange for all other things is determined by the relative difficulty of obtaining them. That a five dollar note of the government of the United States, having no intrinsic value; five silver dollars, having an intrinsic value of something like two dollars and a half; and a five dollar gold piece, having an intrinsic value of five dollars, will exchange in this country for each other or for the same amount of commodities or services, is because the difficulty of getting these things, the quantity and quality of exertion ordinarily required to obtain them, is precisely the same. Should it become in the slightest degree harder to get one of these things than the other, and this will show itself in a change of the rate at which they exchange. In this case we say that the one commands a premium or that the others bear a discount.

What gives to the paper notes or coins of small intrinsic value the same exchange value as the gold coin is that the government concerned, which has a monopoly of coinage in its respective country, will not issue one of them on any less terms that it does the other, thus making them all to the individual equally hard to get.

Chapter 6 — The Two Kinds of Money

While value is always one and the same power, that of commanding labor in exchange, there are, as we have seen, two different kinds of value — that which proceeds from production and that which proceeds from obligation. Now money is peculiarly the representative of value — the common medium or flux through which things are exchanged with reference to their value, and the common measure of value. And corresponding to and proceeding from this distinction between the two kinds of value, there are, we find, two kinds of money in use in the more highly civilized world today — the one which we may call commodity money, originating in the value proceeding from production; and the other, which we may call credit money, originating in the value proceeding from obligation.

This distinction has of course no relation to differences on denomination, such as those between English pounds, French francs and American dollars. These are but differences of nomenclature. Nor yet does it coincide with differences in the material used as money, as for instance that between metal money and paper money. For while all paper money is credit money, all metal money is not commodity money. What I understand by commodity money is money which exchanges at its value as a commodity, that is to say, which passes current at no more than its "intrinsic value," or value of the material of which it is composed. Credit money is money which exchanges at a greater value than that of the material of which is composed. In the one case the whole value for which the money exchanges is the value it would have as a commodity. In the other case the value for which the money exchanges is greater than its commodity value, and hence some part at least of its exchange value as money is given to it by credit or trust.

For instance, a man who exchanges ten dollars' worth of wheat for a coin containing ten dollars' worth of gold makes in reality a barter. He exchanges one commodity for an equal value of another commodity, crediting or trusting nobody, but having in the coin he has received a commodity which, irrespective of its use as money, has an equal value to that which he gave. But the man who exchanges ten dollars' worth of wheat for a ten dollar note receives for a commodity worth ten dollars what, as a commodity, has only the value of a bit of paper. What renders him willing to take it as an equivalent of the wheat is the faith or credit or trust that he can in turn exchange it as money at the same valuation. If he drops the coin into the sea, he loses value to the extent of ten dollars, and the sum of wealth is lessened by that amount. If he burns the paper note, he suffers loss to the value of ten dollars, but he alone; the sum of wealth is not decreased. Paper money is in truth of the same nature as the check or order on an individual or corporation except (and in this lies the difference that makes it money) that it has a wider and readier credit. The value of the coin of full intrinsic value, like the value of the wheat, is a value that comes from production. But the value of the paper money is, like the value of the check or order, a value from obligation.

The first money in use was doubtless a commodity money, and there are some countries where it is still the principal money, and places perhaps where it is the only money. But in the more highly civilized countries it has been superseded by credit money. In the United States for instance, the only commodity or intrinsic value money now in circulation is the gold coinage of the United States. Our other coins have an intrinsic or commodity value that is far less. That they circulate at the same value as the gold coins shows that their exchange value has no reference to their intrinsic value. They are in reality as much credit money as is the greenback, the difference being that the stamp, which evidences their credit and thus secures their circulation, is impressed not on paper, but on a metallic material. The substitution of what is now the cheapest of metals, steel, or the utter elimination of intrinsic value, would not in the slightest lessen their circulating value.

*Now, as soon as the great laborsaving invention of money supplants barter, it is readily perceived that to leave it to every one who chose to do so to issue money would be to entail general inconvenience and loss, to offer many temptations to roguery, and to put the poorer classes of society at a great disadvantage. These obvious considerations have everywhere, as society became well organized, led to the recognition of the coinage of money as an exclusive function of government. The evils entailed by wildcat banking in the United States are too well remembered to need reference. The loss and inconvenience, the swindling and corruption that flowed from the assumption by each State of the Union of the power to license banks of issue ended with the war, and no one would now go back to them.

I think it may be accepted as a principle proved by experience, that any considerable interest having necessary relations with government is more corruptive of government when acting upon government from without than when assumed by government.

It is evidently the business of government to issue money. Yet instead of doing what every public consideration impels them to, and assuming wholly and fully as the exclusive function of the general government the power to issue paper money, the private interests of bankers have compelled the people of the Untied States to the use of a hybrid currency, of which a large part, though guaranteed by the government, is issued and made profitable to corporations. The legitimate business of banking — the safekeeping and loaning of money, and the making and exchange of credits, is properly left to individuals and associations; but by leaving to them, even in part and under restrictions and guaranties, the issuance of money, the people of the United States suffer an increase in the influences which exert a corrupting effect upon their government.

* *These last three paragraphs are taken from George's* Social Problems *(1883), Chapter 27. — L. D.*

Afterword: The Science of Political Economy: What Henry George "Left Out"

by Lindy Davies

In the prefatory note to the original edition of *The Science of Political Economy,* Henry George, Jr., who edited his father's unfinished work, said that the author's original intention had been to create a "'Primer of Political Economy" that would "set forth in direct, didactic form the main principles of what he conceived to be an exact and indisputable science, leaving controversy for a later and larger work." However, George's plan changed, because of the great mass of confusion regarding the basic terms and concepts of the discipline, which had intensified since the publication of *Progress and Poverty.* George exhaustively explored and debunked the standard definitions of terms such as wealth, capital and distribution, and the standard explanations of such economic principles as "the law of diminishing returns in agriculture".

In fashioning a version of George's text for use by modern students, a great deal of material, dealing with notions current in George's day, could profitably be removed. His list of the various contradictory definitions of wealth by long-forgotten economists offers little to today's general reader. Likewise, his long discourse on the meaning of space and time, while interesting as an overview of philosophical currents of the 1890s, does little to elucidate economic principles today. Henry George believed that all this disputation was essential to comprehensively making his case. But when his topical wrangling is stripped away, what's left is an astonishingly simple elaboration of the basic principles of economics — something very much like the sort of "primer" that George originally wanted to write!

Originally, I intended to create an afterword that offered

an "update" of a work that could not have been expected to deal with all the problems of the ensuing century. I wanted to suggest, in other words, an outline of how George might have altered his textbook, had he visited the Earth again in the 21st century. However, as I proceeded with the abridgment I realized that I was making the same sort of mistake that the academic establishment has always tended to make regarding George's work. We find none of today's economic buzzwords in *The Science of Political Economy;* however, George also had little to say about the buzzwords of his own time, except as examples of underlying confusion. As a "primer of political economy", George's work still stands. If one uses it as the author intended, as a "template on which emerging details can be coherently arranged"*, it can offer the modern student a great deal of insight into contemporary questions.

To demonstrate this, I want to briefly discuss some pressing questions for modern-day economics which, though they aren't mentioned in *The Science of Political Economy*, are elucidated by the analytical system it sets forth. The ones I'm thinking of (though others could easily be brought forward) are externalities, environmental policy, business cycle theory (and its relationship to the economic role of government), and globalization.

Externalities

"Externalities exist", writes Paul Samuelson, "when private costs or benefits do not equal social costs or benefits." Thus, exter-

* *Mark Solms, in* Scientific American, *May 2004, referring to the role of Darwin's theory in modern molecular genetics — and, though it had long been thought otherwise, the role of Freud's ideas in modern neuroscience. It is widely contended that Henry George's theoretic contributions, despite having long been held in disrepute, must eventually assume their proper place as just such a template for economic science.*

nalities can affect aggregate outcomes without changing individual incentives. The fact that externalities have become a big area of concern in contemporary economics might reflect a response to the neoclassical emphasis on individual behavior — on aggregate phenomena being understandable as the sum of individual choices. That methodology makes externalities a thorny problem. We cannot say the whole is the sum of its parts if the parts affect the whole in ways that cannot be seen by examining the parts themselves. Therefore, external costs (or benefits) are seen as being outside the marketplace.

Henry George's characterization of the "greater leviathan" of the "body economic" alerts us to the fallacy in the above statement. If external costs are costs, then how can they be outside the marketplace? They are paid by somebody, regardless of whether they appear in any formal accounting of transactions. George's analysis is helpful here because he understands the economy to be the aggregate of all production and distribution, whether denominated or imputed, over the table or under it. Hence, externalities are part of the marketplace, regardless of any official action to "internalize" them. If the government were to step in and impose penalties, that would merely bring those costs back within the comfort zone of quantifiability.

George, however, has the classical preoccupation with the entire economy, or the "wealth of nations" — and it's easy to see that externalities, far from being a new postmodern wrinkle, are a natural and essential part of that analysis. The way that people take advantage of the benefits of civilization is, essentially, by producing wealth and exchanging it. In the laws of production and distribution that George describes, the producer bears the cost of the factors of production, and enjoys the benefits — wages and interest — while the community gets the value it created: economic rent. In George's view, these natural laws of distribution cannot be broken; if human arrangements unwisely go against them, the consequences will inevitably be seen in subsequent production patterns.

In other words, those unwise human arrangements are externalities. External costs are imposed on labor and capital in the form of high rents (which include the speculative increase in the cost of land, plus interest on the money that must be borrowed to acquire land at that price) and confiscation, via taxation, of some of the produce of labor. External benefits are bestowed upon the landowner in payments for benefits that are due to the activity of the entire community. Although economists tend to describe externalities as though they arise mysteriously from some well of market complexity, these, anyway, are directly attributable to arrangements of human law. (And there are many other, lesser examples of legislated externalities, such as the results of zoning regulations, farm subsidies, protective tariffs, etc.)

For Henry George, the question of externalities, and what to do about them, is profoundly simpler than it is for the modern mainstream economist. This is because, for George, the moral basis of property cannot be separated from economic analysis; land is inherently different from wealth. Many pooh-pooh this as merely a moral judgment. But the difference between natural opportunities and the products of labor is so obvious that it can only be denied by an explicit effort to define it away. Natural opportunities are the stuff from which our satisfactions must come, and human labor the means by which our desires can be satisfied. The mixture of the passive element of land and the active element of labor creates wealth — something essentially distinct from both. Since land is not produced by labor, any income that comes from owning land must be an externality.

If there were no natural principle of ownership, and ownership merely stemmed from an ever-changing social contract, then we could not expect predictable consequences to arise from mucking about with those natural principles. Yet they do. The imposition of absolute private ownership of land distorts the processes of production and distribution in ways that have long been understood.

For the mainstream economist, the problem of externalities is far more complex. Denying the possibility of any sort of "natural law of property" — and steadfastly refusing to consider the character of land as a separate factor of production — the mainstream economist is compelled to evaluate each externality afresh, without any guidance except for empirical studies of market behavior. This could lead on the one hand to an excess of regulatory interference, or on the other to a "social Darwinian" impulse to leave things alone to equilibrate. (It also requires major mental gymnastics in the effort to imply — if not actually prove — that land value is not an externality but somehow arises from the landowner's business acumen.)

Environmental Policy

Environmental policy is largely seen in terms of externalities. Firms benefit from spewing greenhouse gases into the atmosphere; foreign debt burdens create perverse incentives to destroy virgin forests and the species they contain; irrigation steals river water from downstream users. But the case-by-case wrangling that characterizes modern environmental policy makes for little progress. Lacking any clear, scientific guide, decisions hinge on a corrupt and/or ill-informed political process. Here, I think, Henry George's political economy has a profound contribution to make.

Henry George affirms the Biblical injunction that "the land shall not be sold forever". That "forever" is important, because it indicates that Georgist political economy, like the Old Testament land law, recognizes the security of land tenure. In fact, George points out that secure tenure is the only way to secure private property in the products of labor. (This lesson has been learned in recent decades by the government of China, which found that privately-owned farms are vastly more productive, per capita and per acre, than collective farms.)

Now this concept — of conditional private property in land — far from being some archaic notion, is clear to anyone familiar with modern laws concerning real estate. In legal terms, "selling a piece of land" is a *non sequitur*. What is transacted is a "bundle of rights" that attaches to a particular site. These rights could include surface rights, subsurface mineral rights, aquifer use rights, air-space rights, etc. When Henry George thundered "We must make land common property!" his fervor and bluntness unnerved some people — but he meant it. George insisted that we allocate the bundle of rights according to the moral basis of ownership. Society must grant secure land tenure, refuse to confiscate the products of labor, and "not sell the land for ever" — by collecting, for society, the socially-created rental value of land.

This simple distinction could go a long way toward solving difficult problems of environmental policy. If the gifts of nature belong to all, then a starting point for environmental policy would be to identify instances in which natural opportunities are being taken for private profit. And if we think of land not just as a square of ground but as a "bundle of rights", we can think of many applications. Northern-hemisphere industrial nations, for example, use the still-uncut forests of the south to soak up their CO_2 emissions. The opportunity to keep their cars and factories spewing with impunity is worth a great deal to them. The cause of that externality is no mystery: the enclosure, for the benefit of a few, of a natural opportunity — in this case, the use of the atmosphere as a dump for a particular quantity of pollution.

It would be rash to say that merely "going Georgist" would make a no-brainer out of environmental policy. A great deal of sorting out would have to be done. For an example of how complex this can get, consider the case of car owners who use the atmospheric commons as a dumping ground for their cars' emissions. They enjoy the benefit of high-performance transportation, yet are only as bothered by pollution as everyone else. Clearly that amounts to the monopolization of a natural opportunity. Wouldn't it be fair, then, to charge car-owners an emissions tax? Perhaps it would be — but there is a whole stew of other incentives to consider. People live and work in a system that virtually requires them to drive a car in order to make a living — because of urban sprawl and the lack of sensible public-transportation alternatives. Furthermore, the sale of automobiles has been actively subsidized by the public provision of highways, cheap fuel, etc. Should individual drivers be penalized for the full amount of pollution that they spew, or should there be some more systemic attempt at reigning in the built-in misincentives? And, if motorists are compelled, because of rush-hour congestion, to wait in traffic, thus increasing their spewage, should they be further charged for this by means of a tax on highway congestion? Could such a tax be administered equitably, or would it just amount to marketing the privilege of using the public highway at the most convenient times? Do not all these real-world complications blow away our happy fantasy of clear-cut Georgist policy decisions?

The fortunate fact is that they do not — or at least, not nearly so much as some would have us think. Trying to evaluate economic phenomena in their moment-to-moment context is like trying to identify scraps of paper in a hurricane. It makes for challenging doctoral thesis topics, requiring ever-subtler mathematical modeling. But in the broad public-policy areas that we are dealing with here — the ones, after all, that are the most important — it isn't necessary. To see why, we have to remember two important facts:

1) Natural opportunities are functionally different from wealth, and can be clearly identified as such. The factors of production are plainly different from each other. Let's imagine factor payments as three colors that get mixed together in the gross receipts of a firm: land is green, labor is red and capital is blue. Mixed together, they become brownish-gray. It's awfully hard to get any of the original colors out. But before they get mixed, Georgist policy calls for the land portion to be taken — while it is still green — and then the entrepreneur's profit can be appropriately purple.

2) Although public policy decisions work through the "body economic" over time in complex ways, Georgist theory reassures us that if those decisions are properly based on "association in equality"* from the start, the resulting interactions will also have that character. Let's consider a (negative) example. At the turn of the 20th century, New York City, responding to its tremendous need to move people efficiently about the city, created a public transportation system (fortunately) before the automobile came into widespread use. The system worked so well that it still carries some seven million riders a day, helping New York City, despite all its other urban problems, to achieve a level of economic dynamism that other cities cannot match. However, the primary beneficiaries of this system — the city's landowners — have not been called upon to pay for it; instead, it is charged to the riders and the general taxpayers. Because rent was not charged to landowners, land

---

* *These are the attributes that George identifies in* Progress and Poverty *(Book X, Chapter III) as fundamental to human progress.*

speculation was encouraged, which retarded the city's economy. Revenue was always a problem, and in time the subway system fell into disrepair. Meanwhile, the (heavily subsidized) national mania for cars and highways threw huge, neighborhood-destroying, revenue-sapping freeways across the city. This is not (necessarily) to say that a sensibly funded and planned city would have no highways at all. But, had the public transportation system been supported as it should have been, by the land rents it helped to create, it could have been provided as a free service, would never have had to suffer from neglect and decay, and would have provided a more viable alternative to highways. Surely that would have made for a more tractable set of urban-planning problems.

A shift to the Georgist paradigm in public revenue will not magically answer all our questions. There are vital debates about, for instance, whether straight land value charges, or severance taxes, or a mixture of both, would be best to secure equal rights to mineral resources, and their efficient use. There are debates over how rights to global resources, such as geosynchronous orbits, or the atmosphere itself, should be assessed and charged. Nevertheless, the fundamental principle that the value of natural opportunities must be collected for common benefit is a powerful de-obfuscatory tool, as useful in the academy as it is at the grassroots.

The Business Cycle

Nowhere is the potential for liberating simplification shown more clearly than in the Georgist theory of the business cycle. This is an area of today's public policy that seems complicated beyond any hope of clarity. There is this bewildering interaction of international balance-of-payments, domestic savings levels, fluctuating currency prices, swinging equity markets, see-sawing rates of unemployment, consumer confidence, geopolitical threat levels and (probably) sunspot activity. For Keynes the business cycle was an inherent feature of the modern economy, a negative by-product of an otherwise highly successful financial system. For Marxists it augurs the eventual fall of capitalism under the weight of its quest for ever-diminishing profits.

Yet George, in setting forth what he deemed necessary for a basic understanding of political economy, never mentioned the business cycle at all! Now, to be sure, he dealt with the question extensively in *Progress and Poverty*; understanding the "paroxysms of industrial depression" was a major focus in that book. He identified the phenomenon of land speculation as the root cause (underlying the myriad proximate causes) of the business cycle, showing how the tendency to boom and bust was merely a special case of the overall problem of poverty amid progress.

The job of political economy, according to George, is to understand the natural laws that govern the production and distribution of wealth. But the business cycle is caused by a refusal to conform society's property relationships to those laws. For Georgists the business cycle is not part of the economic organism, but rather a disease — a chronic disease, to be sure — yet one that can be fully cured. To the extent that the annual value of natural opportunities can be collected, and taxes on labor and capital abolished, the problem of the business cycle can be solved. That's why *The Science of Political Economy* "fails to mention" the business cycle, except as an example of the consequences arising from interference with the distribution of wealth.

What, then, does this say about the role of government in a system informed and corrected by Georgist principles? Here again, there is little need for the "basic primer" to go into specific cases when the guiding principle is so clearly stated. Rewards attributable to labor and the products of labor go to those who provide the service; rewards attributable to natural opportunities or to the entire community's activities go to the community. (The rent fund always directly affects the community's vitality and health: either positively, as when it is collected and used for common benefit, or negatively, as when it is left in private hands and a syndrome of social pathologies results.)

There is a certain class of activities, often called "natural monopolies", whose value is created by the action of the State. George recommends that such enterprises, which by their nature do not permit competition, should be operated by the government. In his other works he discusses various examples of these things, but in *The Science of Political Economy* he focuses on one only: money. This is because other monopolies come and go with changes in time and technology, but money is an essential part of political economy.

For George, "bad money" (i.e., money with less intrinsic value) drives out "good money" because the fundamental usefulness of money is to save labor in the process of exchange, and it takes less labor to provide credit money than commodity money. He notes many historical examples in which the debasement of currency has led to ruinous inflation. But, he reasons, currency can easily be debased — in fact its commodity value can be utterly removed — without any harmful effects, if only its supply is kept carefully regulated. This leads us to realize that the most efficient way for currency to be issued is by government fiat. If any profit is to be gained from issuing money, it should go to the general treasury, and not to private banking interests. In other words, the essential nature of money indicates that, at a sufficiently advanced stage of civilization, it must be issued by government.

There is considerable disagreement, even (or perhaps especially) among advocates of Georgist policy about the precise role of money in society and how to secure a just, stable supply of the stuff. Nevertheless, it is clear that the beacon of the natural law of property as a fundamental guiding principle can bring us far closer to the goal of comprehensibility in questions of public policy. It allows us to evaluate the role of government in terms of basic principles, rather than merely as month-to-month crisis management.

Globalization

Today's "anti-globalization movement" responds with something very much like panic to the economic realities of our time. And well it might: the "internationalization of production" seems to come along with a host of frightening problems: the erosion of wages and regulatory standards, the disappearance of habitats and species, the possibility of irreversible climate change, corporate predation of workers in nations struggling under the burden of foreign debt, the decline of labor unions, the decline of manufacturing in the United States. Understandably worried as folks are, though, most are not clear on the causes of these problems. The increasing fact of a "global economy" frightens people — but why, exactly? International trade has been going on for centuries, despite persistent attempts to choke it off (to benefit some special interest) via tariffs or blockades. Lately, improvements in transportation and communication have made it easier for producers to move parts of their operations overseas — but can technological progress be blamed for today's economic woes? After all, both international trade and technological progress have the potential to increase production with the same amount of exertion, or to achieve the same level of satisfaction with less damage to the environment. Yet those things are not being done: why? "Because the corporations are in control" is the next common answer. "Corporations use their henchmen in the WTO to erode national sovereignty and become more powerful than nations. They skim off all the benefits for their richest one per cent, leaving everyone else worse off."

This is true; income and wealth are becoming more polarized all the time. Yet one wonders how the corporations manage to seize regulatory control from the grasp of sovereign nations. The standard answer is that in today's "global economy" a nation must — in order to be able to sell its goods abroad — play by international-trade rules that are set by the corporations. A nation that tries to stick with minimum-wage, worker safety or environmental regulations will not be able to compete in the "race to the bottom" with other countries that are even more desperate.

It ought to be pointed out, though, that not one of these "desperate" national governments has taken advantage of its power to resolve the underlying, fundamental problem of poverty — which it shares with every other nation in the world today. That is the secret of the "merry-go-round" that no country can seem to get off of. Every player in the "global economy" today allows individuals and corporations to own land in fee simple, and every nation imposes taxes on labor and capital. In addition, many of the world's nations struggle under a burden of foreign debt, contracted by earlier regimes, almost never with the people's say-so. The borrowed money was mostly squandered, and the debts, which ballooned as the United States fought to contain inflation in the early 1980s, are essentially unpayable. Yet in return for "debt relief", nations must impose "austerity" — further cutting back on needed investment in infrastructure, education and public health.

It is this pattern of fundamental injustice, and the inefficiency it brings about, that is really at the heart of what people see as the "death force" of globalization. Once again, Georgist political economy furnishes a guiding principle that allows us to make sense of a wide range of seemingly disparate effects — and provides clear policy alternatives. Indeed, if a few nations were to succeed in implementing Georgist public revenue policy, they could begin a "domino effect" far greater than the "red menace" nightmares of the old cold warriors. This outcome would be good for workers and producers, but disastrous for the special interests that currently run the show — which provides even more support for Prof. Mason Gaffney's contention, in *The Corruption of Economics,* that even now, a large part of the intellectual power of mainstream economics is spent on making sure that these guiding principles, in all their powerful simplicity, do not become widely understood.

Lindy Davies is the Program Director of the Henry George Institute. He has been teaching political economy since 1988, and has written, edited, designed and implemented numerous curricular materials in that effort. He is the webmaster for www.henrygeorge.org and www.landreform.org.

INDEX

D

E

N

Made in United States
Orlando, FL
04 November 2026

90205474R00173